1995

Conversations with Robert Graves

Literary Conversations Series

Peggy Whitman Prenshaw
General Editor

Conversations
with Robert Graves

Edited by
Frank L. Kersnowski

University Press of Mississippi
Jackson and London

Copyright © 1989 by the University Press of Mississippi
All rights reserved
Manufactured in the United States of America
92   91   90   89   4 3 2 1
The paper in this book meets the guidelines for permanence and durability of the Committee on
Production Guidelines for Book Longevity of the Council on Library Resources.

Library of Congress Cataloging-in-Publication Data
Graves, Robert, 1895-
    Conversations with Robert Graves / edited by Frank L. Kersnowski.
        p.   cm. — (Literary conversations series)
    Includes index.
    ISBN 0-87805-413-8 (alk. paper).—ISBN 0-87805-414-6 (pbk. :
alk. paper)
        1. Graves, Robert, 1895- —Interviews. 2. Authors,
English—20th century—Interviews. I. Kersnowski, Frank L., 1934-
. II. Title. III. Series.
PR6013.R35Z464   1989   89-32216
821'.912—dc20   CIP

British Library Cataloguing-in-Publication data is available.

Books by Robert Graves

Over the Brazier. London: Poetry Bookshop, 1916.

Fairies and Fusilers. London: Heinemann, 1918.

The Pier-Glass. London: Secker; New York: Knopf, 1921.

On English Poetry. New York: Knopf; London: Heinemann, 1922.

Whipperginny. London: Heinemann; New York: Knopf, 1923.

Poetic Unreason and Other Studies. London: Cecil Palmer, 1925.

Lawrence and the Arabs. London: Cape, 1927.

A Survey of Modernist Poetry (with Laura Riding). London: Heinemann, 1927.

Goodbye to All That: An Autobiography. London: Cape, 1929. Rev. ed. New York: Doubleday; London: Cassell, 1957.

The Shout. London: Matthews and Marrot, 1929.

I. Claudius. London: Barker; New York: Smith and Haas, 1934.

Claudius the God and His Wife Messalina. London: Barker; New York: Smith and Haas, 1935.

Antiqua, Penny, Puce. Deya: Seizen Press; London: Constable, 1936.

Collected Poems. London: Cassell; New York: Random House, 1938.

The Long Week-end: A Social History of Great Britain 1918-1939 (with Alan Hodge). London: Faber and Faber, 1940.

The Story of Marie Powell: Wife to Mr. Milton. London: Cassell, 1943.

King Jesus. New York: Creative Age Press; London: Cassell, 1946.

The White Goddess. A Historical Grammar of Poetic Myth. London: Faber and Faber; New York: Creative Age Press, 1948.

The Transformation of Lucius, Otherwise Known as the Golden Ass by Apuleius (translation by Robert Graves). London: Penguin, 1950.

The Nazarene Gospel Restored (with Joshua Podro). London: Cassell, 1953.

The Greek Myths. 2 vol London and Baltimore: Penguin, 1955.

Pharsalia; Dramatic Episodes of the Civil Wars by Luccan (translation by Robert Graves). London: Penguin, 1956.

The Twelve Caesars by Suetonius (translation by Robert Graves). London: Penguin, 1957.

They Hanged My Saintly Billy: The Life and Death of Dr. William Palmer. London: Cassell, 1957.

Collected Poems 1959. London: Cassell, 1959.

Oxford Address on Poetry. London: Cassell, 1961.

Collected Short Stories. New York: Doubleday, 1964.

The Hebrew Myths: The Book of Genesis. New York: Doubleday; London: Cassell, 1964.

Mammon and the Black Goddess. London: Cassell; New York: Doubleday, 1965.

Difficult Questions, Easy Answers. London: Cassell, 1972.

Collected Poems 1975. London: Cassell, 1975.

In Broken Images: Selected Letters of Robert Graves 1914-1946 (edited by Paul O'Prey). London: Hutchinson, 1982.

Between Moon and Moon. Selected Letters of Robert Graves 1946-1972 (edited by Paul O'Prey). London: Hutchinson, 1984.

Contents

Introduction

Robert Graves was born into a stable and intellectually accomplished Victorian family. His mother, Amy, came from an affluent family that valued both the arts and scholarship, and throughout her life, she supported Robert's endeavors—often financially. Alfred Perceval Graves, his father, who was active in the Irish Literary Society and achieved considerable renown for his own writing, encouraged Robert's writing and helped him place poems for publication. Through his father Robert met Lloyd George and, indirectly, T. E. Lawrence. The family expected that Robert would go from public school to Oxford and then to an academic career, continuing and elevating their accomplishments. And so Robert might have done if World War I had not revealed the startling inhumanity of the machine age: ugly and ignoble deaths in the trenches, shell shock and battle fatigue that destroyed hope and personal stability, and the actions of war profiteers.

Robert's response, expressed pointedly in the title of his autobiography, *Goodbye to All That* (1929), was to reject all that he regarded as both insubstantial and insincere, especially the beliefs of the Victorian world of his parents. Yet between the time he was commissioned in the Royal Welsh Fusiliers in 1914 and the time he wrote his autobiography, he married, fathered four children, received his B. Litt. from Oxford and accepted a teaching position in Egypt. He was closely associated with Edward Marsh and the Georgian poets, publishing in *Georgian Poetry*. Though the Georgians were young poets who intended to invigorate the poetry of their day, their acceptance of the tastes and values of educated classes defined the nature of their poetry. Graves also became a part of the group gathered around T. E. Lawrence, the hero England needed after the devastation of World War I. Graves seemed a personality unlikely to adopt a nontraditional life.

In fact, his most unprecedented act had been leaving his wife and living with Laura Riding. In 1969 he told me that he had gone with

Laura Riding because his wife wanted him to, suggesting a reliance
on feminine will he would celebrate in *The White Goddess* as the
basis of culture in western history. Even in rejecting the standards of
the Victorian world, Graves looked for historical precedent and never
appealed simply to the gratification of personal desire. Having left
England with Laura Riding, he might well have been expected to
settle in bohemian Paris. He and Laura Riding did in fact visit France
but, at the suggestion of Gertrude Stein, moved to Mallorca, not to
the main city, Palma, but instead to the village Deyá placed between
the mountains and the Sea. This was in 1929. For almost sixty years,
he would live there as often and as much as war, his writing, his
family and his friends would allow. Robert Graves was a happy
village dweller, whether in England, Wales or Spain. Probably the
histories of the inhabitants and the traditions of the villages, known to
all who lived there, met his need for personal honesty in his own life
and the pursuit in his writing of truths he could believe in without
qualification. Unquestionably, being with Laura Riding was central to
the life Robert Graves chose to live; for she was a woman of strong
will, great talent and unrelenting intellectuality. Yet Robert Graves was
with Deyá a lifetime longer than he was with Laura Riding.

When I was in Deyá in 1969, the village was simple even then in
its amenities: two hotels and two cafés, perhaps an Abbot and
Costello film outdoors every week or two. The small, pebbly beach
certainly couldn't compare with the splendid beaches on the main-
land. Yet Robert Graves chose to live and write there. As evidenced
by many of the pieces in this collection, many of the world's
important and famous went out of their way to Deyá to see him, as
did many more with unremembered names.

Many of the visitors heard the same stories, were asked the same
questions and probably wondered why they had made such a trip
only to stand dumbly in the company of a man who chatted easily
with the children around him who only knew him as Robert. Many of
the writers in this collection have given answers to the "why," and
most would probably agree with what George Steiner wrote in "The
Genius of Robert Graves," published in *The Kenyon Review* (1960):

> To get the full flavour of the man one must have had the privilege of
> seeing him in his home on the island of Majorca (a privilege of which a

growing number of young poets, disciples and would-be biographers are availing themselves annually). The setting is incomparable: bastions of rock shading from copper to pastel gray with the passage of the sun; gnarled olive trees and orange orchards descending in escarpments to secluded coves; and all-surrounding the Mediterranean, here perhaps more time-haunted, more daemonic and legend-like than anywhere else. The villagers, who speak an ancient and difficult language, will point out "Senor Graves' " house with reticent pleasure. He is one of them and that is something few foreigners have ever achieved in a Spanish community.

It is true that Graves's presence, more so than is true of many writers, affected his readers. But the power of Graves's writing was the essential lure for one to travel to Deyá to visit him. What those who conducted formal interviews with Graves at his home in Deyá achieved eludes simple rational explanation.

Many of Graves's prose works have introduced radical ideas. *Goodbye to All That, The Story of Marie Powell: Wife to Mr. Milton, The Greek Myths, The White Goddess, King Jesus, The Rubiayyat of Omar Khayaam*—in all Graves seems disputative, challenging. Without doubt, he was. Yet to see the books only so is as limited as to see Graves simply as a village dweller. In his books, and in almost all of his poetry, Graves opened discussion with people past and present who, like him, were concerned with the origin and nature of culture and society. To see Graves in Deyá added another dimension to the man revealed in his books, but the visit could not replace the books.

Such was the man that to meet Graves was to accept what he said, in part because his openness made him appear incapable of deception. Dannie Abse in "A Meeting with Robert Graves" did not question his being on familiar terms with Prime Minister Heath. I in turn did not question that he was a son of the Prophet when he told me so. In part we accepted the truth of Graves's statements because of the way in which he included someone in his constantly changing circle of friends and acquaintances: some people simply were welcome and others were not. Those who were welcome had relationships of varying complexity with Graves, and most had the same components. They responded to Graves's publications in conversations, letters and reciprocal publications. The relationships were not simply based on eating olives and drinking wine. Ideally, they were not based on the books alone without the presence of the man. Yet the books on their own have outlived the man.

He wrote over 120 books, revised his poetry continuously and carried on a very extensive correspondence, mostly by hand with pen and ink. Even for a man who lived to be 90, such writing—and the accompanying research—would seem to have left little time for adventure. There are no accounts of hunting trips to Africa or passages on the great ocean liners and luxury trains, no stories of brawls in famous cafes or loud disputations in restaurants. In fact, after the battles and the wounds of World War I and the much talked about episode with Laura Riding (during which each jumped from a window), little that might be termed action occurred in Graves's life. At least, no accounts at present exist, though the authorized biography when written, may well revise the current understanding. The first volume *Robert Graves: The Assult Heroic 1895-1926*, published in 1986, revealed that Robert Graves did travel a great deal, especially to Eastern Europe, in the service of poetry.

Perhaps because we have no evidence to the contrary, Graves's life appears simply to be that of a man who lived on a remote island and wrote books that caused a great many people to want to meet him. The appeal of the books themselves, even such as *The White Goddess* with its exceedingly complex arguments, is both emotional and intellectual. *The White Goddess*, as much as any of his books, established Robert Graves as an unavoidable voice in the story of poets and poetry in this century. There the dominance of the woman is asserted, as is the importance of the muse. For Graves love between poet and muse, usually unavoidably physical, could never be permanent. Perhaps his early interest in Freudian thought led him to look for the value of relationships, even ones beyond acceptance, without condemning them. Or perhaps Graves is right: the matriarchy is the original and natural structure of human society, and *The White Goddess* moves readers because of its truth. Whatever the answer, *The White Goddess* is of central importance to Graves's writing and has been, as well, an explanation of human behavior that has offered a most persuasive answer to the riddle of love and poetry.

Especially in the sixties and seventies, Graves became a cult figure because of his openness to drugs and extramarital sex. But he continuously reminded those who wanted another guru of the counter culture that he did not approve of promiscuity and the indiscriminate use of drugs. Predictably, the cults and their gurus ran their course. And Graves remained on his island. Magus rather than guru for younger writers, Graves argued—as he had earlier with T. E. Lawrence—that poetry resulted from a way of life rather than verbal dexterity. And when he was referred to as "the old master" by younger poets the praise was of a life that produced the poetry. See, for example, *Between Moon and Moon*, the second volume of Graves's selected letters, and its letters and references to Kingley Amis, Ted Hughes, and many others. His influences reached also such goddesses of the screen as Gina Lollobrigida and Ava Gardner.

His was a complex and full life, as of yet barely sketched in, even though Martin Seymour-Smith revealed much in *Robert Graves: His Life and Works* (1982). But what we have seen, what is confirmed by the pieces included in this volume, is that the public facet of Graves's life showed a man who was myth as much as mythographer, a man whose writing explained and celebrated his need for the anguish of love and the endurance of a woman who loved. He needed as well Deyá, made sacred by Robert Graves's devotion.

The interviews and essays in this volume are reprinted uncut and uncorrected in spelling and punctuation. Since Robert Graves was asked similar questions by many reviewers, he often replied with similar, or identical, answers. This repetition has been retained since it forms part of very distinct portrayals of Graves and its exclusion would detract from the accuracy of the views. Graves emerges from these pieces as a man with his roots and genius tied firmly to place, a man certain of his purpose, and passionate in its execution.

There are people to thank for their help in this book's coming to life: Seetha Srinivasan of the University Press of Mississippi for patiently answering all my questions; Linda Shaughnessy, Robert Graves's agent, and William Graves, son of Beryl and Robert Graves, for their constant advice; relatives, especially my wife, and friends, expecially Skip Eno, who have listened and commented—again patiently.

And then there is Robert Graves, to whose memory this book is dedicated.

FK
January 1989

Chronology

1895   Born 26 July 1895 to Alfred Perceval Graves and his second wife, Amalie (Amy) Elizabeth Sophie von Ranke, at Wimbledon, England

1910–14   Attends Charterhouse

1913   Meets Edward Marsh, editor of *Georgian Poetry*

1914   Meets Robert Frost

1914–18   Officer in the Royal Welsh Fusilers; seriously wounded at the Battle of the Somme

1915   Meets Siegfried Sassoon

1918   On 23 January marries Nancy Nicholson; they have four children: Jenny Prydie Nicholson, John David Graves, Catherine Nicholson, Samuel Graves.

1919   Meets Richard Hughes

1919–21   Rents Boars Hill cottage from John Masefield

1920   Meets T.E. Lawrence at All Souls College, Oxford

1922   Begins correspondence with John Crowe Ransom; develops friendship with Edith Sitwell.

1924   Wins Silver Medal for Poetry at Summer Olympic Games

1925   Awarded B. Litt degree from St. John's College, Oxford;
          considers writing a critical study with T.S. Eliot; meets
          Virginia and Leonard Woolf.

1926   Meets Laura Riding Gottschalk

1926–27   Professor of English Literature at the Royal Egyptian
          University in Cairo

1928   Begins Seizen Press with Laura Riding

1929   Moves to Mallorca with Laura Riding at the suggestion of
          Gertrude Stein

1932   Moves into Canellūn in Deyá

1935   Wins Hawthornden Prize for *I, Claudius*

1936   Leaves Mallorca because of the Spanish Civil War

1939   Moves to America with Laura Riding; returns to England;
          Laura Riding remains in America with Schyler Jackson,
          whom she marries in 1941.

1939–46   Lives in Devonshire, England

1941   Meets Joshua Podro

1946   Returns to Deyá

1949   Divorced from Nancy Nicholson

1950   Marries Beryl Pritchard; they have four children: William,
          Lucia, Juan, Tòmas.

1953   Refuses appointment of Commander of the Order of the
          British Empire

1954–55 Delivers Clark Lectures at Cambridge

1957   Meets E.E. Cummings; meets W.H. Auden.

1959   Receives Gold Medal of National Poetry Society of
         America; visits Israel at the government's invitation.

1960   Meets Idries and Omar Ali Shah

1961–66 Oxford Professor of Poetry

1962   Refuses honor of being named Companion of Literature
         by the Royal Society of Literature

1968   Visits Hungary and the Soviet Union; awarded Gold
         Medal for Poetry, Cultural Olympics; awarded Queen's
         Gold Medal for Poetry.

1969   Becomes the only "adopted son" of Deyá

1970   Visits Hungary at the invitation of the PEN Club and
         establishes there the Robert Graves Prize for Poetry

1971   Visits Hungary again

1973   Visits Hungary and Poland

1976   *I, Claudius* is a BBC Television series; visits Poland again.

1978   Last visit to England

1985   Dies in Deyá on 7 December 1985

Conversations with Robert Graves

Retreat from Parnassus

Peter Quenell/1920

From *The Sign of the Fish*. (London: Collins, 1960), 32-36.
Reprinted by permission.

With one of these rustic poets, nevertheless, I presently formed a
stimulating friendship, not a friendship that was destined to last but,
so long as it lasted, of unusual value. Robert Graves was then living
at Islip, a stone-built village close to Oxford; and when I went up to
the University to sit for an examination at Balliol, I and my father,
although he distrusted poets, whom he suspected of being drunken
and promiscuous, left the grim outskirts of North Oxford and walked
to Islip across the riverine fields. On our way, I remember, we were
much troubled by the shameless conduct of a pair of lovers, who
flung themselves on to the meadow grass and proceeded to engage
in carnal lovemaking before we were fairly out of sight. "Couldn't
they *wait?* . . ." muttered my father furiously—he had naturally a
very pure mind; and their behaviour seemed a bad omen for our visit
to an unknown bohemian poet, whom we might well discover living
in concubinage, surrounded by an illegitimate brood. But, although
the poet's manner struck him as "rough", and his corduroy suit was
rougher still, Robert Graves impressed my father as being probably a
"decent sort of fellow", with a fresh-cheeked and unaffected wife—
curiously insistent, however, on being addressed by her maiden
name: she turned out to be a passionate feminist who regarded the
adoption of one's husband's name as a mark of matrimonial servi-
tude—and a number of wholesome noisy children running wild
around their small house. Neither of them "drank", my father
noticed; the food they provided was plain and sensible; and Graves
appeared to love the country and take some interest in the local
antiquities, a subject about which my father was always prepared to
talk at length. Meanwhile I was studying the writer's appearance—a
nose broken like that of Michelangelo, and thick dark hair that curled
on his forehead like the locks of Michelangelo's *David*, together with

3

a sallow skin and a mobile, slightly twisted mouth. It was clear that he was a remarkably affectionate parent, and he told us that a poet ought to write seated in the middle of his family, while he minded a fractious child or kept his eye upon a bubbling saucepan. His view of life, at the time, was still intensely puritanical; and he even asserted that a "bad man"—bad in the accepted moral sense—could scarcely hope to be a good artist. This was a statement that my father found unexpectedly reassuring.

Once I had gone up to Oxford, I made a habit of revisiting Islip, and Robert Graves would pay me flying visits in my overheated rooms at Balliol. Flying—for he arrived on a bicycle and was always hurried though always good-tempered, carrying a heavy knapsack full of groceries and vegetables, which, as soon as he had smoked a cigarette, he must immediately shoulder and trundle home. The cigarette came from a big expensive box—aromatic "Balkan So-branies"—much more expensive than I could rightly afford, but bought on credit at the College stores. I had already begun to develop a dangerous taste for worldly luxuries; and the austerity of the poet's ideals and the honest bleakness of his domestic surround-ings provided a useful corrective to the silliness and wanton frivolity of youth. Robert Graves also supplied some valuable ideas about the art of writing. His theories had not yet solidified into a dogmatic critical system. The fearsome White Goddess had yet to ascend her throne; and his remarkable literary partnership with Laura Riding—a pale mop-headed young woman who reached London, while I still knew him, as Laura Riding Gottschalk—was not to be established and proclaimed until he and I had both left Oxford. At the moment, the influence he felt most strongly was that of the fabulous Lawrence of Arabia; and Lawrence's opinions, often wildly erratic, he distrib-uted broadcast to all who listened. There were only three French poets, he once informed me—Villon, Baudelaire—he had forgotten the name of the third. Where had he learned this, I cautiously asked him. Lawrence had said so, he replied, as he hoisted his knapsack between his shoulders.

On the other hand, if he spoke from his own experience, the ad-vice that he gave was usually sound. The poet, he once remarked, must always be careful in his use of colour-adjectives. A mere versifier was apt to employ them lavishly—his productions blushed and

beamed like a bad picture of a tropical sunset; whereas the true poet
rarely introduced a colour, and then only at a point where it greatly
heightened and enriched an image. Did I remember two poems by
Donne, each of which contained a single mention of a colour, so
aptly and unexpectedly placed that it seemed to flash from the sur-
rounding lines?—the sixteenth *Elegie*, addressed to his youthful
mistress—

> Nor in bed fright thy nurse
> With midnight's startings, crying out, Oh, Oh
> Nurse, O my love is slain, I saw him go
> O'er the *white* Alps alone . . .

—and *Elegie V*, imagining his return to her arms after an adventurous
voyage overseas—

> When weather-beaten I come back; my hand
> Perhaps with rude oars torn, or sunbeams tann'd . . .
> My body a sack of bones, broken within,
> And powder's *blue* stains scatter'd on my skin . . .

Such were the conclusions of a modern who studied his art as
thoroughly and diligently as a cabinet-maker or a master-mason; but
his point of view was already distinguished by a certain touch of
genial crankiness, which he owed (his biographer may decide) to an
interesting combination of ancestral strains. On his mother's side, for
example, he was descended from erudite German stock: on his
father's, related to a Cromwellian regicide and an eccentric eighteenth-century clergyman, author of *The Spiritual Quixote*. The
seventeenth and the odder regions of the eighteenth century were, I
have often thought, his proper background; and I could imagine him
producing one of those gigantic volumes, in the same tradition as the
works of Browne, Burton or Henry More, the "Cambridge Platonist",
where a poetic will-o-the-wisp flutters ahead of the reader's footsteps
through an endless forest of curious learning, occasionally coming to
rest on some fantastic branch or twig. Later, he was to publish a
quantity of books, in which he revised the New Testament or cast
strange sidelights on Classical mythology, and was to advocate a
method of scholarly research entitled "analeptic thinking", which, so
far as I have been able to discover, encourages us first to decide what

we wish to believe, then look around for scholarly evidence to give
our intuitive convictions a decent measure of support. But at Islip the
Quixotic man of learning had not yet definitely taken control. He was
as vulnerable as he was easily impressionable, and still exhibited the
wounded features of a shell-shocked public schoolboy, who had gone
straight from Charterhouse to a line regiment, had been shot through
the body on some Flemish battlefield and temporarily left for dead.
In common with many survivors of the battle, he wore the strained
and troubled expression of a young man who had lately emerged
from an inferno.

27 April 1925

Virginia Woolf/1925

From *The Diary of Virginia Woolf, 1925-30*, vol. 3, ed. Anne Oliver Bell (New York and London: Harcourt, Brace and Janovich, 1980), 12-14. Reprinted by permission.

Monday 27 April

The Common Reader was out on Thursday:[1] this is Monday, & so far I have not heard a word about it, private or public: it is as if one tossed a stone into a pond, & the waters closed without a ripple. And I am perfectly content, & care less than I have ever cared, & make this note just to remind me next time of the sublime progress of my books. I have been sitting to Vogue, the Becks that is, in their mews, which Mr Woolner built as his studio, & perhaps it was there he thought of my mother, whom he wished to marry, I think.[2] But my present reflection is that people have any number of states of consciousness: & I should like to investigate the party consciousness, the frock consciousness &c. The fashion world at the Becks—Mrs Garland was there superintending a display—is certainly one;[3] where people secrete an envelope which connects them & protects them from others, like myself, who am outside the envelope, foreign bodies. These states are very difficult (obviously I grope for words) but I'm always coming back to it. The party consciousness, for example: Sybil's consciousness. You must not break it. It is something real. You must keep it up; conspire together. Still I cannot get at what I mean. Then I meant to dash off Graves before I forget him.[4]

Figure a bolt eyed blue shirted shockheaded hatless man in a blue overcoat standing goggling at the door at 4.30, on Friday. "Mrs Woolf?" I dreading & suspecting some Nation genius, some young man determined to unbosom himself, rushed him to the basement, where he said "I'm Graves". "I'm Graves". Everybody stared. He appeared to have been rushing through the air at 60 miles an hour & to have alighted temporarily. So he came up, &, wily as I am, I knew that to advance holding the kettle in a dishclout was precisely the

right method, attitude, pose. The poor boy is all emphasis protesta-
tion & pose. He has a crude likeness to Shelley, save that his nose is
a switchback & his lines blurred. But the consciousness of genius is
bad for people. He stayed till 7.15 (we were going to Caesar &
Cleopatra—a strange rhetorical romantic early Shaw play[5]) & had at
last to say so, for he was so thick in the delight of explaining his way
of life to us that no bee stuck faster to honey. He cooks, his wife
cleans; 4 children are brought up in the elementary school; the
villagers give them vegetables; they were married in Church; his wife
calls herself Nancy Nicolson; won't go to Garsington, said to him I
must have a house for nothing; on a river; in a village with a square
church tower; near but not on a railway—all of which, as she knows
her mind, he procured. Calling herself Nicolson has sorted her friends
into sheep & goats. All this to us sounded like the usual self
consciousness of young men, especially as he threw in, gratuitously,
the information that he descends from dean rector, Bishop, Von
Ranker &c &c &c: only in order to say that he despises them. Still,
still, he is a nice ingenuous rattle headed young man; but why should
our age put this burden of proof on us? Surely once one could live
simply without protestations. I tried, perhaps, to curry favour, as my
weakness is. L. was adamant. Then we were offered a ticket for the
Cup tie, to see wh. Graves has come to London after 6 years; cant
travel in a train without being sick; is rather proud of his sensibility.
No I don't think he'll write great poetry: but what will you? The
sensitive are needed too; the halfbaked, stammering stuttering, who
perhaps improve their own quarter of Oxfordshire.

And on Sunday we had our first walk, to Epping.[6]

[1]*The Common Reader* was published by the Hogarth Press on 23 April in an edition of 1250
copies (*HP Checklist* 81).

[2]Maurice Adams Beck (1886-1960) and his partner Helen Macgregor were *Vogue*'s chief
photographers at this period. Their studios at 4 Marylebone Mews had been built in 1861 at the
rear of his new house at 29 Welbeck Street by the pre-Raphaelite sculptor Thomas Woolner
(1825-1892), who about that time had sought leave to make a bust of Julia Jackson, for whom
he cherished 'a more than artistic admiration', and to whom he made an offer of marriage; both
overtures were declined. (See Leslie Stephen, *The Mausoleum Book*, edited by Alan Bell,
1977, p 28.) Beck and MacGregor had photographed VW the previous year, and one was
reproduced by *Vogue* in its feature 'We Nominate for the Hall of Fame' in late May, 1924 (see
also *In Vogue*, edited by Georgina Howell, 1975, p 61). A portrait from the present sitting was

to appear in *Vogue*'s early May issue, 1926. (See also *QB II*, pl. 6a; Cecil Beaton, *British Photographers*, 1944, p 61.)

3Madge Garland was Fashion Editor of *Vogue* under Dorothy Todd's editorship.

4Robert Ranke Graves (b. 1895), poet and novelist; in 1918 he had married eighteen-year-old Nancy, daughter of the painter William Nicholson. The information concerning Graves's heredity and way of life here summarised by VW is amplified in his autobiography *Goodbye To All That* (1929). The Hogarth Press had already published two, and were to publish a further four, books by him (see *HP Checklist*, nos. 33, 46, 59, 63, 92 and 93).

5Bernard Shaw's play, with Cedric Hardwicke and Gwen Ffrangcon-Davies in the name parts, was given by the Birmingham Repertory Theatre Company at the Kingsway Theatre; the Woolfs went on the evening of 23 April—a Thursday, which implies that VW was mistaken in supposing Graves's visit to have been on a Friday.

6Of this outing LW noted in his diary: 'Went Loughton train, & walked Epping Forest, High Beech & Chingford, & back by bus.'

An Evening in Maida Vale
Julian Symons/1937

From *The London Magazine*, 3:10 n.s. (January 1964), 34-41.
Reprinted by permission.

Though more is quoted from Laura Riding than from
Robert Graves in this essay, the portrayal of Graves's
relationship with Laura Riding is too important to exclude.
In fact, her dominance of the conversation indicates the
nature of the relationship, one which has been seen by
many as anticipating Graves's fascination with powerful
women figures—such as the White Goddess.

One brightly cold May evening twenty-five years ago I climbed the
steps of a house in Maida Vale, and used the knocker. The door was
opened by Robert Graves, who welcomed me genially, but I thought
a little nervously. He took me into a large drawing room. 'Sit down,
sit down,' he said. 'Miss Riding will be here in a moment. Would you
like some beer?'

How, how and why, is it possible to separate one distant evening
from another? Why has this after-dinner visit stuck in my mind clear
in almost every detail, when so many other occasions, just as eagerly
anticipated, are rolled into one great ball of eating and drinking and
conversation? Partly because of the admiration I felt for the poetry of
Laura Riding, no doubt, and because this was the only time I met
her; partly because of the evening's farcical results: but I cannot help
feeling that there is some richer and deeper explanation for the way
in which this evening stays in my mind, fixed like a series of stills from
a film symbolizing some of the fears and hesitations, the attitudes and
ideas, of the thirties.

Perhaps a word of elaboration would be useful. The *Survey of
Modernist Poetry*, written in collaboration by Laura Riding and
Robert Graves, was the first critical book about 'modern' poetry that I
read, in my teens, and I accepted it as a guide for differentiating what

was real from what was fake in the poetry of the time. Later on I
picked up second-hand her first book of poems, *The Close Chaplet*,
published under her given name of Laura Gottschalk, and was fascinated by poems like 'The Definition of Love' (the book appeared in
1926):

> The definition of love in many languages
> At once establishes
> Identities of episodes
> And makes the parallel
> Of myth colloquial. . . .
>
> Love to love, like man to man,
> Is not speech but the error
> Of ancestor to now
> Instead of now to now
> And ancestor to ancestor.

Later I still read *Epilogue*, the fat twice-yearly magazine which they
issued from their home in Majorca. Admiration did not stop me from
enjoying Roy Campbell's squib in *The Georgiad*:

> Inspire me, fun, and set my fancy striding.
> I'll be your Graves, and you my Laura Riding.
> Or since my metaphor has set you frowning,
> That other Robert and his missus, Browning.

When I began to gather contributions for an American number of
Twentieth Century Verse, I wrote to ask her for a poem. She was
known to be an opponent of all anthologies, and I was not surprised
when her reply was by no means so welcoming as those of Allen
Tate, R. P. Blackmur, Yvor Winters, Delmore Schwartz and others.
She would want to know, she said, something more about this
American number before contributing to it. What poems were to
appear, in what order, who was to write an article about American
poetry which I had mentioned, what would be said of her own
poems in it? This was the sort of letter that I should have answered
pretty sharply had it come from almost anybody else, but I was
prepared to regard Miss Riding in the way she regarded herself, as a
special case. I replied with a brave long list of possible contributors,

which included the names of T. S. Eliot, Wallace Stevens and Conrad
Aiken. (In the end Stevens and Aiken sent poems, Eliot didn't.) At
the time I was naïve enough to think that this list might be persuasive,
but in fact my catalogue of names probably produced an effect
almost the reverse of that I intended. With the over-optimistic list I
sent, for a reason I cannot now remember, some of my own poems.
By way of reply, Miss Riding invited me to come and see her. We had
a telephone conversation, and here I was.

I had not long to wait. She came in, wearing a dark dress reaching
almost to the ground, and using a stick to help her lameness. She
was in her late thirties, and beautiful in a ferocious way: sharp nose,
thin lips, eyes dark and snapping. The immediate impression of intellectual acuity was reinforced by her incisive voice. Her first words
after greeting disconcerted me a little.

'You are not very tall,' she said. As a six-footer I was surprised.
What had she expected? But she amplified this at once, although not
in a way that increased my understanding, by saying, 'You are not so
tall as you sounded on the telephone.'

I made no reply. Now Graves, who had been in the room with us,
retired, and our conversation began. He played on this evening the
part of a supernumerary, popping in and out frequently to see what
progress we were making or to bring me another bottle of beer, his
entry usually marked by a question, sharp in effect although not in
words.

'What do you want, Robert?'

'I am taking letters down to the post. I am looking for some
stamps.'

That was one exchange, and I remember another, because of the
constant humming literary activity that it seemed to indicate.

'What are you doing now?'

'I have almost finished a chapter. Then I shall come in.'

At last he did come in, and came to stay. That, however, was after
we had been talking—or, for the most part, Laura Riding had been
talking and I had been listening—for some hour and a half.

We did not talk much about the proposed American number,
although that was the ostensible reason for my visit. I wanted simply
to get between covers samples of the work of the American poets I
admired, particularly because most of them (Stevens, for instance)

were hardly known in England at that time. I gathered, without her saying it in so many words, that such an idea seemed to her deplorably catholic and unprecise. The American number was soon replaced as a subject by my poems, which were anatomized line by line, phrase by phrase, with a skill and sharpness that for a time quite overwhelmed me. I do not mean that I objected to it, or would have objected if I had known in advance what was going to happen. Few writers dislike hearing their work seriously discussed: but still, while I was conscious of the honour done me, and aware of the intellectual skill with which the dissection was carried out, there was something oppressive in Laura Riding's certainty of tone. She took my poems to pieces (as, I am sure, she had taken to pieces many better poems) not exactly in the way of the New Critics, who were then little known and certainly not in the sociological way that I myself favoured, but considering them rather as verbal entities which had been written to express some specific moral feeling.

'What you really meant to say in this verse,' she would say, 'was. . . .' Had I meant to say just that? I did not feel sure of it, but her own certainty was impressive. When I raised objections she was ready for me. 'But don't you see that what you are saying now is inconsistent with your opening lines? They say one thing and now you are saying another. There is a confusion of thought.'

Only at one point, I think, did I positively argue with her. A verse in one poem ended

Nor can deduce from years
A year's hypoteneuse

She pounced upon this. 'A year's hypoteneuse. Now, what do you mean by that?'

I began to explain. 'Yes,' she said. 'But that is hypotenuse. You have written hypoteneuse. Don't you see that the difference of sound implies a considerable difference of meaning? If hypoteneuse was in your head, if you felt that was the sound of the word, then it must have affected the whole poem.'

She rejected out of hand the explanation that I had made a mistake in spelling, but the exact import of my writing hypoteneuse was left unresolved. As we went on talking, I was conscious of an increasing area of disagreement. I have always preferred the cut and thrust

of argument to the wittiest or most instructive monologue, and her
talk tended more and more to sweep aside my comments and objections. Although I did not voice the emotional restiveness I felt—
indeed, in my memory we stayed fixed in our positions for this hour
and a half like flies in ice, she enforcing the thrust of her voice by an
occasional darting glance from her dark eyes and producing on me
rather the effect of the Wicked Queen in *Snow White*, I making occasional play with my beer—I was rather glad when Robert Graves, his
chapter finished, came in.

The conversation became general, although still literary. I mentioned the name of John Crowe Ransom, whose work had been
introduced to this country by Robert Graves. Miss Riding observed
that his view of Ransom's work had changed considerably, and
Graves agreed. There was, indeed, not much room for disagreement
with her. I said that I admired Auden, and at this there was a good
deal of head-shaking, of an almost medical kind. A course of therapy
was suggested. It would be a good thing, perhaps a real eye-opener
for me, if I talked with a young friend of theirs who was writing an
article about Auden. I agreed to do so, with an uneasy feeling that I
was undergoing some sort of test which I was pretty sure to fail. I
brought the talk back to my American number, without much result.

The young friend, whom I had better call X, asked me to dinner.
We had a pleasant evening, and he outlined his ideas about Auden.
In general, these—which were held at the time by people outside the
Graves-Riding circle—were that Auden's work owed very much to
Robert Graves and even more to Laura Riding, and that his talent
was almost wholly imitative rather than original. In the course of making a line by line analysis of Auden's poem on Spain, X had discovered that the opening lines were an almost direct transcription from a
travel book. Would I care to co-operate in the work of analysis? I said
rather firmly that I wouldn't.

X was warm and friendly—in Laura Riding's ambience I had been
aware of what might be called a natural chill—and, led on by drink
and a game of darts I was, not for the first or the last time, indiscreet.
I told that baffling little story about my being not very tall and,
prompted by gentle questions from X, went on to talk about Laura
Riding. What impression had she made on me? X asked, and I answered very much what I have written here. Among many admiring

words I dropped the fatal poison of two critical ones: her personality was, I said, aggressive, and the total effect of her conversation was rather wearing.

X nodded gravely, and made no comment. When I had left he passed on these words, and the whole substance of our conversation. There ensued a tremendous correspondence. I had, as Laura Riding made plain to me in a slightly regretful letter, failed the test. Why had I not said that I found her discussion of my poems wearing? At the first hint of this she would have stopped talking about them, and we could have gone on to something else. She explained, although hardly to my satisfaction, the remark about my not being tall, which X had dutifully passed on with the rest. On the telephone, she said, my voice gave an impression of pomp half a mile long, and she had been genuinely surprised, and pleased, to find me not so long. Perhaps, she added, she should have said long, not tall.

X weighed in with a little self-justification. 'I do not think I have complicated negotiations between you and her, because obviously if you really feel that she is aggressive the negotiations would be bound to be unsatisfactory, I have really presented you with an opportunity to make clear your feelings about her before matters became complicated by co-operation between you and her.' Negotiations, complications, co-operation: I felt myself becoming entangled in an extraordinary emotional web from which it was essential that I should cut free. It will be remembered that the degree of co-operation involved was simply that she should send me a poem which, it need hardly be said, she now thought it 'inappropriate' that she should do.

It would be tiresome to recount in detail the triangular correspondence that followed, in which she regretted that I was a frivolous rather than a serious person and insisted upon the absolute frankness that must exist between friends, and X emphasized the purity of his motives, while I accused them both of taking casual remarks too seriously. But this correspondence was not the end of a situation lingering, as Laura Riding put it, between reality and unreality. A few months later she wrote to me about a long review I had written of her collected poems; wrote, while controverting some of the points I made, with friendliness. But I was not to stay for long in the sun of her approval. When, by another rash stroke, I sent her a review of her work written by Hugh Gordon Porteus and published in *Twen-*

tieth Century Verse, she fired at me a reproachful volley. How, holding the view of her work that I did, could I publish a piece that she thought silly, stupid and shameful? A public apology was the only thing that could set the record straight, she suggested, and I never made it.

Even that was not quite the end of the affair. She had lent me a book by the poet Robert Fitzgerald, and now she asked for its return. When I took the volume from the shelf I saw with horror that I had written my name in it. I felt that such an act was certain to appear in a bad light. I bought a bottle of ink eraser and tried to remove the offending name, but either the ink was of peculiar power or I used the eraser inefficiently, for the result of my operation was to leave a great illegible smear on the fly-leaf. Did this look like some sort of devious insult? I am afraid it may have done.

I have suggested that this evening in Maida Vale had a symptomatic as well as a comic interest. My purpose in recounting it is not to make any sort of judgement of Laura Riding. Her exercise of her art, and her conception of conduct, represented an aspect of literary life in the thirties that is now too little recognised: the tendency towards extreme individualism and poetic isolation. The opposite tendency, which regarded the poet as one more worker bee in the hive, and which permitted extreme freedom of action and comment in private relations while insisting on a strict public social morality, has been well enough understood and publicized—and it was very much to this view that I adhered myself at the time; but the isolationist attitude, with its insistence on purity in poetic speech and an accompanying close finickiness in personal relationships, is ignored or forgotten. Laura Riding made, better than anybody else, a statement of this attitude:

> 'I became a poet because I was filled with hopes of human good, but could see no room for my hope except in the isolation of poetry. . . . Poetry was for me a form of living, a state of being in which the redemption of human life from its deadly disorder by truth could be looked forward to. Although I had no company in that state, I sustained myself in it in the happy certainty that there was a destined fulfilment of common humanity in truth. . . . My whole art was an anticipation of the intonations of truth; thus my word-style had a peculiar rectitude of accent.'

Her style had more influence, and influence over more poets, than is commonly granted now. On Auden, Graves and Norman Cameron her influence was obvious and profound, but many other poets benefited, some of them indirectly, from her virtuous tight rectitude, her utter elimination of what she called in one letter to me 'marzipan' and in another 'the luxury-stab we are taught to look for at school'. Her determination to purify language, so that the words used in poems should be simple and perfectly accurate, led in her own writing to the rejection not merely of luxury-stabs but of the whole colour and movement that is normally associated with poetry. The remarkable long poem, 'The Vain Life of Voltaire', which she wrote at the age of twenty, the pieces in her first book, *The Close Chaplet*, and another long poem, 'The Life of the Dead', written in the early thirties, all have a richness, a waywardness, a conscious pleasure in the sensuous nature of words, that is missing more and more in the last poems she published, at the end of the thirties.

By that time she had perhaps come to regard rather forlornly the attempt to form an emotional community of virtuous individuals. Her most ambitious and as it seems now most curious, attempt to do this was embodied in a book called *The World and Ourselves*, published early in 1939, in which sixty-five more or less notable people attempted to answer the question, 'What can be done about the outside disorders of our time from the inside?' Her own belief was that 'the true intelligences of the world' must co-operate and 'separate themselves from the mass in order to be of use to it'.

She did not find many to share this belief, and shortly after this book's publication she came to doubt whether it was possible ever to use words purely enough for the writing of poetry.

'My words were still the words of a careless tradition of speech, and their intractability as such drew me ever closer to the crux of the human problem: the question of the validity of words.'

Just as the only perfectly pure painting is the blank canvas, so the only perfectly pure poem is that which does not use words, as we recognize them today, at all: this was the logic of her position, and it was a logic she accepted. During the fourteen years between 1925 and 1939 her literary activity was considerable and various: poems, critical essays, stories as simple and enigmatic as fairy tales, came from her pen. The best of these now almost unobtainable books are *Anarchism is Not Enough* and *Experts are Puzzled*, but they are all plainly the work of an extraordinary talent, unlike anything else written in this century. When, in 1939, she decided finally that all words were impure, she wrote no more.

It is hard to avoid a note of comedy in writing about her—and indeed why should one avoid it? Yet that is not the note to end on in considering her achievement. It was not possible to talk to her without appreciating the power of her intellect, the self-destructive simplicity of her mind. Her Jewish tailor father hoped that she would become an American Rosa Luxemburg. She became instead (so long a silence permits a valediction) a sort of saint of poetry and, like all saints, tiresome: but what she did, by her work and her example, to purify poetic language, could have been done in no other way, and perhaps by no other kind of person. There are many who owe her a debt.

Where Truth Begins

T.S. Matthews/1949

To preserve the sense of continuity in the discussions between Graves and Matthews, I have omitted passages that do not directly concern the relationship between the two men.

Robert was not the most businesslike of men. He trusted anyone whom he considered his friend and, to put it mildly, his taste in people was catholic. He himself was quixotically generous, even when he could not afford to be. Long before he became what he considered "affluent," he owned four houses in Deyá: Canellun (which he had built) and C'an Torrent; the Posada, next to the church, and a small house on the path down to the *cala*, both of which he had bought. With these houses went several acres of valuable olive trees. The Posada, a large-ish house, and the one on the path to the *cala* could have been let, but Robert used them instead as guest houses for visiting friends.

In 1945, when the war was over, Robert returned to Mallorca, with Beryl and their three children, William, Lucia and Juan. Everything at Canellun was just as he had left it nearly ten years before. His hat was hanging on the same peg, his stick was leaning in the corner, all his books and papers were in order. On the table in the hall a shallow bowl still held the varicolored pebbles he had put there.

Robert had left all his property and belongings in the care of his trusted Mallorquin friend, Gelat, the factotum of Deyá, whom I have described earlier. Robert was touched by this evidence of trustworthiness and at the same time delighted by the vindication of his own judgment—like a gambler who thinks he has won his bet not because

he is lucky but because he knows the winning system. Since Spanish
Law forbade foreigners to own land outside a village, Canellun and
its land were in Gelat's name. Gelat could have kept everything, but
was satisfied with the land, a small parcel of which his heirs
eventually sold back to Robert.

Was Gelat really the faithful friend Robert thought him, or did he
intend to hang on to this windfall? The possibility may have occurred
to him. In any case, at his death the title went to Gelat's son Juan as
part of his father's estate. That one was a jovial character, unlike his
father: he laughed heartily at the idea of restoring Robert's property,
which was now legally his. Juan did not try to turn Robert out of Canellun, but while this unpleasant business was going on, and while
three of the children were at school in Palma Robert rented a dreary
flat in the outskirts of Palma, and there he and his family lived for
several years.

I visited Robert and Beryl and the children—now four: the baby,
Tomas, was my namesake—crammed into their flat (actually two
flats) on a characterless street. The household also included a young
English couple, Martin Seymour-Smith and a girl whose name I have
forgotten; they didn't live in Robert's flat but had a workroom there.
Seymour-Smith acted as tutor to the two oldest children, and he and
the girl were doing the spadework for Robert's biggest potboiler yet,
The Greek Myths.

It was on this visit that Robert introduced me to the works of
Georges Simenon, a writer he much admired. Before I left on the
night boat to Barcelona, we were all having dinner at a restaurant on
the waterfront in Palma. The talk was mainly of writing and writers,
and not a name was mentioned without being scornfully dismissed as
an overrated fake. This began to annoy me, and at last I said, "Who
is any good?" Robert looked at me in surprise, and then he and the
others started to draw up a list of writers of whom they approved. It
was a short list: E.E. Cummings and Simenon. Nobody else.

The process of Robert's self-delusion (as I thought it) was a gradual
one; but I saw it coming, and even made an attempt, halfhearted and
too late, to warn him against taking himself too seriously as a solver
of historical riddles. I say that "I saw it coming," but of course
that's only true in a sense. I couldn't help noticing that whenever he
got on the subject of Mediterranean mythology he showed himself

violently hostile to the gods of Olympus, whom he characterized as usurpers, and was an equally violent partisan of the Mother Goddess, the head and front of "the old religion," the true faith that, according to him, had been driven underground by the Greek gods. His mystical and reverent attitude towards the Mother Goddess was only explicable, I thought, in the light of his long thraldom to Laura and his worship of her—a thraldom and a worship whose effects on him were permanent.

To Robert the orthodox version of the Greek myths was an attempt to cover up or give a false interpretation to the older myths that lay behind them, and he set himself the task of peeling off the top layer of this palimpsest and restoring the faint traces of the original. Pure scholarship would have been unequal to this job, since too much evidence was lacking. Robert undertook to supply the missing evidence, either by setting the scholars at naught and reinterpreting what they had misunderstood or by imagining the nature or even the form of the missing facts.

As he worked his way around the coasts and islands of the Mediterranean, I asked myself what would happen when he reached the eastern shore. It was too much to expect that he could bear to overlook or refrain from setting straight the myth of Christianity, with all its conjectural facts, wrong guesses and false conclusions. I feared the worst. And I remember the first indication that my fears were well founded.

It was in the summer of 1949; we were having a reunion, the first and last of its kind, at Portofino. Our hosts were Robert's oldest daughter Jenny and her husband Alex Clifford, who owned the Castelletto, surely one of the most beautifully placed houses in the world. The Castelletto stands on the highest point of the headland, 900 feet above the sea, overlooking Portofino's miniature harbor and the hillsides behind it, the Bay of Rapallo and the whole sweep of sea towards Spezia on one side and San Fruttuoso and Genoa on the other. Most of the house itself is carved out of the solid rock, with two turret-like rooms—an octagonal living room and a spare bedroom—emerging from the walled terrace that is also the roof of the house below. The path to the Castelletto is half an hour's climb from the village (twenty minutes for a native), and all luggage and supplies have to be carried up.

Jenny had a room for Julie and me in the Castelletto itself; the

boys stayed at the Nazionale, a small hotel on the village square; and
Robert and all his family were in a house about halfway up the hill.
Jenny was an indefatigable and efficient hostess, and for the three
days of our stay there was a continuous round of lunches, cocktail
parties and dinners. Robert was in great form. He announced happily
that this was the first time he had ever been in Italy—in spite of all he
had written about the Romans—and that he liked it.

After one of the lunch parties at the Castelletto Robert produced a
typescript which he wanted me to read then and there. I saw by the
title that it had something to do with one of the New Testament para-
bles. I took it back to my room to read. I think (but can't be sure) that
the parable in question was the one about the unjust steward; I do
remember that Robert had recast it so that the moral was just the
opposite of what it had been. Robert's assertion was that he had
restored the parable to its original and proper form; that the reason
why it had come down to us in a corrupt version was that some
enemy had tampered with the original manuscript and had turned
the meaning of Christ's words upside down.

This was the first hint I had of Robert's dawning interest in a new
crossword puzzle, the Christian religion, in which he was not only
going to fill in all the blank spaces but correct many of the accepted
answers. I didn't want to get into a public argument with him that
might end in a quarrel or at least bad feeling. So when he asked my
opinion all I would say was that I preferred the original version.

We were given a farewell lunch *al fresco*, the whole party sitting at
a long table on the piazza in front of the Nazionale. I sat next to
Robert, who was not feeling well and had little to say. But at one
point he turned to me with his characteristic sigh and said,

"I don't think you could ever do anything I would really mind."

I was surprised and touched. "Why, Robert," I said, "what makes
you think that?"

"*I* don't know."

Robert supported a sizable family—actually two families (Nancy and
her four children, then Beryl and another four)—not to mention
numerous friends and hangers-on, by his pen alone. He had only
one salaried job in his life, and that one lasted only a year: the professorship of English at the Egyptian University, Cairo. He must have

written as many million words, or thereabouts, as Georges Simenon or Edgar Wallace, but the scope, quality and variety of his writing were far beyond theirs.

Robert Graves must be allowed, as a writer who has tended his trade "with uncessant care" (though his own god will judge how strictly he has meditated the thankless Muse), to be among the most experienced and accomplished of his generation, who long ago left far behind such would-be teachers as Laura Riding. When it comes to writing "clean English," as he calls it, no one can do it better; and in the craft of verse, within his carefully circumscribed limits, few have excelled him. Like Arnold Bennett, he would tackle any question, and he became so seasoned a craftsman that he could turn out a competent job of writing on any subject he chose.

I still remember an epitaph he wrote for his son-in-law's grave-stone. Alec Clifford, who married Robert's eldest daughter Jenny, was one of the best British war correspondents in the Second World War, and his foreign correspondence after the war was the brightest feather in the *Daily Mail*'s cap. It was Alec who found and rebuilt that marvelous Castelletto at Portofino, where he and Jenny staged our last reunion with Robert in 1949. Julie died later that year, and Alec lived only four years longer: he too died of cancer (Hodgkin's disease) but kept on working till a month or two before his death. This was the epitaph that Robert wrote for him:

OF THOSE CHARGED TO WITNESS VIOLENCE & MISERY

FEW HAVE LEFT

SO TRUTHFUL AND COMPASSIONATE A RECORD.*

That revised parable Robert had shown me in Portofino was only a beginning, as I had suspected. The next time I saw him was in Deya in the early 1950s—my first return there since Julie's death. Robert had published *King Jesus*, his fictional account of the life of Christ, and was working on a more serious and ambitious book, *The Nazarene Gospel Restored*. On one of our walks he said to me,

"This book I'm doing now. It frightens me."

"Why, Robert?"

"Because I have a kind of sentimental attachment to the Church I

---

*The accepted idiom "charged with witnessing" would require five more letters: I suppose Robert was forced into this negologism by limitations of space.

was brought up in, and this book will destroy the Church. It's like having the responsibility for dropping the atom bomb. Christianity will be finished."

"Finished? Now, Robert!"

"Yes, finished, *kaput*. Oh, it may not happen overnight, and everywhere at once. The Catholics will go on telling themselves fairy stories—it may not affect them much. But Protestant Christianity will be wiped out. The only refuge Protestants can find will be to become Jews—and Pharisees at that."

How much of this did he really believe? It's impossible to say; but it was obvious that he had begun to take his "findings" seriously, and was evolving a technique of "historical research" that would enable him to discover anything he set out to find. He was like a dowser searching for water, except that he needed no forked stick: he could tell the approach of his quarry, as surely as the witch in Macbeth, by the pricking of his thumbs.

From time to time I have reviewed books by Robert; although then the reviews in *Time* were anonymous, he knew I had written them. I think he must have subscribed to a clipping bureau, for he seemed to read all the reviews of his books, and it became his settled practice to write a letter of protest or correction to the editor whenever he thought the review inaccurate or unfair. Over the years I must have reviewed five or six of his books without rousing his ire, but at last in 1958 I did it.

The book, called *Five Pens in Hand,* was a collection of miscellaneous articles and lectures: not a very good book, but like all Robert's writing, except when he was being a solemn scholar, very readable. This was my review:

> Robert Graves is a prose writer of nimble prejudices, coaxing imagination and gap-toothed flashes of disarming charm. He is an old professional who takes care to write cleanly, and his signature is always recognizable. He wishes to be considered, and will probably be remembered, as primarily a poet—a good poet, but not a "great" one (a term which he hates and whose validity he denies).
>
> He will also be remembered, I think, as the author of *Goodbye to All That,* surely one of the best autobiographies ever written and one of the few first-class books about World War I. (A revised version has recently been published in England and America.) And what other writer of our day—with the possible exception of Simenon, who is not

in the same class—has shown such unfailing gusto in getting the work out? By his own estimate his "old-fashioned steel nib" has written more than four million words.

His latest book will lose him no friends (he and the Apostle Paul would never have hit it off, in any case) nor, I should think, have much effect on his secure standing as a wit, an accomplished story teller and a grizzled *enfant terrible* among the scholars . . . .

When George Moore wrote *The Brook Kerith* he proved himself an "ignorant old rascal," but nevertheless did base his book on "three bold and accurate guesses: . . . that Paul willfully misrepresented Jesus; that Jesus survived the Cross; and that he then considered himself to have offended God by 'forcing the hour.' " Yet, even while Mr. Graves is flying through the air with the greatest of ease, he acknowledges that he does hear an occasional low whistle from skeptical observers: "Scholars speak very cruelly of my work sometimes, accusing me of wild guessing."

He does more. He confesses, in so many words: "My imagination is not that of a natural liar, because my Protestant conscience restrains me from inventing complete fictions; but I am Irishman enough to coax stories into a better shape than I found them." Now, how can you resist that? It's like the Chekhov character who sighs and says: "When I philosophize, I lie terribly." And when Mr. Graves is chuckling out a story, not a complete fiction, but jollied into a better shape than he found it, or writing about himself as if he were the character that indeed he is, there's no denying him. . . .

The book includes twenty of his latest poems (none from my favorite drawer) which speak, as always, for themselves. It also includes a story he says is "ancient," though it was new to me: "An old lady was taking a pet tortoise by train, in a basket, from London to Edinburgh, and wanted to know whether she ought to buy a dog-ticket for it, as one has to do in England if one takes a cat by train—because cats officially count as dogs. 'No,' said the ticket inspector, 'No, mum! Cats is dogs, and rabbits is dogs, and dogs is dogs, and squirrels, in cages, is parrots; but this here turkle is a hinsect. We won't charge you nothing, mum!' "

This here turkle is a hinsect.

My review was intended to pull Robert's leg, but not too hard, about his method of historical dowsing, to which there were several references in this book; I headed the review "This Here Turkle Is a Hinsect." Shortly afterwards Robert wrote me:

Read your review in the N.Y. *Times*. If you feel obliged to prove so convincingly that our friendship does not prevent you from speaking your mind, why go out of the way to review my books? I'm not angry in the least, only curious. I love you dearly. But you do the god-damnedest things sometimes and reduce me to falling back on my superiority-complex . . . .

He said that he himself made it a rule never to review a friend's book unless he could speak only good of it. My suggestion that he cheats is all the more damaging since I'm known to be his friend. None of the points I raised in my review should have been made "to excite ridicule." Why not try to prove him wrong?—that would be more to the point and more helpful.

And he signed himself "Puzzled."

I replied:

Oh, Robert, Robert!

You *were* offended. I'm sorry. But you really shouldn't have been. I've read the review over, anxiously, and got Martha to read it again too. We both think you're being a little prickly.

I've reviewed books of yours before (though never again) and much more critically, and not a word out of you. Whatever faults can be found with this review, it was certainly friendly, and must have been taken so by everyone who read it—though not, obviously, by you.

Tom

I didn't leave it at this, however. A month or so later I was going to Ibiza with friends. Ibiza was only a few hours by boat from Mallorca, so I wrote to Robert and proposed myself for a two-day visit. Before that I had heard from him again:

Thanks for your affectionate letter. Why I wasn't offended by your review of *King Jesus* was that it was offered as fiction; and in fiction one has licence to rearrange events; as also in poetry. But to suggest that a historian takes liberties with his facts is to call him a liar. . . . I don't mind being called crazy, self-opinionated, etc., etc. but if the people to whom you showed your review don't think that it matters whether one tells the truth or not they must be very cynical or even something worse.

Anyhow, everything is straight now I hope. Do *please* come & see us. Much love from us all.

So I went to Canellun for a couple of days, and all was well again. Robert and I went for a walk and talked out our differences—at least to the extent of my promising that I would not review any more of his books. The second day, on another walk, he said, "By the way, have you seen a book of mine called *Five Pens in Hand?*

I looked at him; he stared, then remembered; and we both laughed.

I Reminded Him of Muggleton

Alan Sillitoe/1955

From *Shenadoah*, 13 (Winter 1962), 47-50. Reprinted by permission.

After a couple of months on Majorca I sent Robert Graves some of my poems, and he wrote back asking me to come over to Deyá one Sunday and have tea. So on the first fine weekend of spring I borrowed a bicycle and pedalled off up the mountian road. Trees in the valley were heavy with lemons and oranges, perfuming the road for much of the way up, and when the last half-dozen loops of it reached the col I was rewarded by a wide horizon of the Balearic Sea. Olive groves and pine trees descended to black giantesque rocks by the shore, holding back a hypnotic gently heaving sheet of blue. When I'd had my fill of it I set off downhill, and went almost to Deyá without pedalling.

The house was easy to find, a grey structure by an elbow of road before the village, built on the proceeds of "Claudius" in the early thirties—when Robert Graves was there with the American poet Laura Riding. I left my bicycle on the garden path, and walked to the back door. It was open, but shielded by a hanging curtain of fine steel chain. No one was in sight. Green shoots showed on the grapevine already, and an assortment of broken toys were strewn around the door: bows and arrows, a dancing shoe, a satchel, and a boy's bicycle leaning against the wall.

"Anybody in?" I called out. The movement of a chair from inside, then footsteps, and two hands parted the chain curtain. Graves stood there, a pair of scissors in one hand and a jug in the other, towering above me—it seemed—so I stepped back to make our different heights less pronounced. He looked quizzical, as if he might have seen me somewhere before and couldn't quite place me.

"Are you Robert Graves?" I asked, breaking the silence. I told him my name, adding that I lived in Soller, and had written to him. He thought for a moment, then said: "I received your letter." He left the

28

jug on the kitchen table, crossed the step and came outside: "I'm going to pick some lemons for lemonade. It's a hot afternoon; how did you get up from Soller?"

"I came by bike, that one by the path. I'll give you a hand if you like."

"All right." We went into the garden, tugging fruit from trees and filling a straw basket. "Some of your poems are good," he said, still looking at me as if waiting for some sort of recognition. "At least you end them well. So many people get off to a good start, then fizzle out half way through, coming in lamely at the end." He was a big man, with grizzled hair, a broken nose (from boxing, he told me), full lips, a vigorous head; he wore sandals, blue jeans, and a brown open-necked shirt—a well-built middle-aged sixty.

We went into the house, the living-room windows overlooked the sea. I asked if he was busy of a Sunday. He poured two glasses of lemonade and sat at the large table covered with books and papers, signing a limited edition of his poems, a light labour that enabled us to talk through the scratching of his signature. "I'm always busy," he replied. "There are no holidays for a writer, especially when he has a large family."

"I find it impossible to work all the time."

"So did I once, but it became a habit. Then it's not so difficult." I asked where was the rest of the family? "Down at the beach," he said, setting the sheets out around him to dry. I relaxed while questions and answers crossed the table at the lazy rate of Sunday afternoon. I said I found his remarks about my poetry encouraging, but that so far none had been published. "That doesn't matter," he replied. "As long as you keep on writing them." This wasn't the sort of truth I wanted to hear: "I'd still like to see them in print."

"That's no problem if you keep writing."

We talked about the various ways in which Ulysses and Telemachus were said to have died—the theme of one of my poems. "Telemachus," he told me (he was then working on the Greek Myths) "was banned from Ithaca by Odysseus, who had been warned that his son would kill him—but it turned out to be another son, Telegonus. In the end Telemachus married Circe," he smiled. "Wasn't that strange?"

We went outside again, into the soft warm air. A few goat bells sounded lazily among the terraces, and nothing else, silence, solitude, as far down as the sea and even beyond. "What part of England do you come from?"

Nottingham: I hadn't seen it for some time, and the word came like a shock, bringing a sudden clear vision of packed streets and factory chimneys, of tar melting between cobblestones in summer, of riotous public houses on Saturday night.

"I've some pleasant memories of Nottingham," he said, "though I've never actually lived there. When we were poor—after the Great War—I received a cheque for a hundred pounds from a Nottingham manufacturer. It was one Christmas and I'd given the postman my last shilling. The man said in his letter that he didn't think poets should starve, and that he hoped the enclosed would help me. That was generous of him, don't you think? Another time I was to go before a medical reassessment board for my pension, and the railway warrant was made out to Nottingham by mistake. I was so ill by the time I got to my real destination that the pension was kept on! I'm sure Nottingham's a town worth writing about, if you're thinking of doing a novel."

From book to book—walking slowly from the roadway up to the house—we got to *The Long Weekend,* a social history of England between the wars, which he wrote with Alan Hodge. He asked if I knew anything about the Nottingham habit of a girl who, saying a loud goodbye to a boy friend late at night after her parents had gone to bed, slammed the house door with the boy friend still on the inside. Of course I knew about it; I said I felt sure it still went on, as it must in other places though. I remembered this Nottingham habit when I wrote *Saturday Night and Sunday Morning.*

Back to the house, a quick exploration on my way up to the lava-tory revealed several small bedrooms whose main furniture seemed to be beds and books. The four children were living there at the time. Sitting down over a drink, Graves still signing his poems, he asked me which university I'd been to. "I didn't go to any," I replied. "I left school early."

"So did I," he said, "I left school to go to the War." Poverty was an important topic: "How do you manage to live out here?" he asked. I told him I had a pension: had been invalided from the Air Force. This

led us to Lawrence and *The Mint.* Lawrence, he said, had been kind
to poets, and in the twenties gave him a first edition of *The Seven
Pillars of Wisdom,* which he said he had been able to sell for three
hundred pounds.

At this point Mrs. Graves came back with three children, and the
table was cleared for tea. During the commotion Graves looked at me
again and suddenly began sorting through a heap of papers on the
windowsill. He took one out and held it up, then passed it to is wife:
"Who does this remind you of?" Both thought it reminded them of
me, and so did I. It was an engraving of Ludowick Muggleton, an
eighteenth-century journeyman-preacher who started the sect of the
Muggltonians in the North of England, said to be still flourishing up to
fifty years ago. "I knew you reminded me of someone as soon as I
saw you," Graves said, pleased with himself for having solved the
riddle.

We sat for some time drinking *conac,* a fiery Spanish brandy that
later helped me on my way back to Soller—flying around the hairpin
bends with more speed than wisdom.

A Talk with Robert Graves: English Poet in Majorca

Arnold Sherman/1956

From *Commentary*, 22 (October 1956), 364-66.

I often saw a towering giant of a man, beyond middle age and usually dressed in an over-sized sweater and dungarees, on the beach near our home on Majorca. Sometimes he was alone, but usually he was accompanied by a slender, studious-looking woman and a blond, blue-eyed boy of two. Although our home was not inaccessible, it was off the beaten track for tourists and so the presence of strangers, and strangers who were undoubtedly foreigners, aroused our curiosity. I saw the "giant" as a retired British colonel, while my wife insisted he was a painter. Finally, we asked a Majorcan native who lived nearby if he knew who the stranger was.

"He is supposed to be an extraordinary writer," we were told, "a very great man who has lived almost all his life here."

"Do you know his name?" I asked, already half suspecting the answer.

"Roberto Graves. Have you heard of him?"

A week later, while I was admiring the pattern the tides had engraved on the beach, Graves appeared from behind a sand dune and, raising his huge arms, dove into the Mediterranean.

When he returned, dripping, to the beach, I approached him. "Is the water cold?" I asked meekly.

"You're an American," he retorted accusingly, not bothering to answer me.

He dried himself by vigorously flapping his hands in the air. "And a writer?"

I blushed and he smiled triumphantly. "I knew it," he said. "I can always spot Americans and I can always spot a writer and the easiest creature in the world to detect is an American writer. They are sometimes impossible people."

Impossible or not, Graves invited me to his home in Palma, Majorca's capital.

Graves, with his wife and the three youngest of his eight children, lived on two floors in an ancient but well-preserved part of the city, where he stays for the three months of the Majorcan winter. The rest of the year he lives in Deyá, a remote village in the northeast of the island.

When I arrived at his house Graves greeted me warmly and led me into his study. Piles of books several feet high stood everywhere in the huge room. Socks, underwear, shoelaces, broken pencils, and sea shells were strewn in every direction. A half dozen manuscripts lay on a desk and hundreds of magazines were scattered over the floor. The only thing that lent a semblance of order to the place was a long bookcase in the rear that held copies of all of Graves's books— over ninety volumes of poetry, criticism, essays, historical novels, and translations from the Greek, Latin, Spanish, and German. Their subjects ranged from the life of Jesus to the reign of Claudius, through the Dark ages and the Renaissance, to descriptions of the island that has been the writer's home for nearly half his life.

"You probably want to know," Graves began, "why I came to Majorca in the first place. Admittedly, this is a rather isolated place for a man whose work so often depends upon painstaking research. There are no libraries here. The island, in terms of certain luxuries, is primitive, and except for a short interlude during which George Sand and Frederick Chopin vacationed here one winter, the island has no real tradition of art. Yet I find it one of the most serene and tranquil spots in the world. There are parts of this island that contain all the beauty that I was accustomed to in Wales as a child, less the bitter climate and provincialism of the latter. The people of Majorca are the most gentle group of individuals in the world. They combine a sense of natural modesty, pride, and honesty in all their dealings. I brought up eight children here and have written over ninety books and hundreds upon hundreds of articles from my home in Deyá and I've never regretted a moment spent here."

His eye turned to two manuscripts lying on the desk before him. "These are two translations that I'm currently working on. They're rather obscure Latin treatises. I try to keep in trim by translating a certain number of books each year. I'm also writing a novel about an Englishman named William Palmer who was hanged in June 1856. I find it very easy to do because the Victorian era was so rich and dirty."

A maid entered and poured the first cup of English tea I had tasted in Spain. "I have a rather difficult question to ask you," I said. "You've practiced nearly every conceivable form of writing, and according to the critics you have more or less succeeded in all of them. But which do you yourself prefer?"

Grave's pale blue eyes began to sparkle. He rose and said emphatically, "I enjoy translating, but of course I am not primarily a translator. By the same token I write novels, but I do that mostly for money. In fact all but one thing I do, I do for fun, exercise, or money. The one exception is poetry. All that matters in all my writing has been poetry. It is the only thing that should matter to a dedicated writer. I don't know how posterity will treat many of the things that I've written in the past, but I am convinced that my poetry will endure.

"One of the disheartening features of our civilization," he continued, "is that men, preposterous men, have succeeded in convincing public and critics alike that they are poets. Dylan Thomas, for example, was an admirable alcoholic, but little else. My good friend T. S. Eliot wrote good poetry, but unfortunately that was over twenty years ago. And then, of course, there is the greatest imposter of them all—Ezra Pound.

"Do you know, many years ago, I was invited to a dinner at which Pound was present. When we were introduced, the host said, 'Robert, I want you to meet Ezra Pound. You and he won't like each other.' Well, not only do I not like Ezra Pound and not only do I regard him as a charlatan and an imposter, but I abhor and refuse to forgive his fascism. Lunatic or not, after the war ended and after he had defended the right of the Nazis to slaughter six million Jews, and of the Italians to wipe out the primitive and helpless Ethiopians, I could not in honesty follow Eliot's example and sign my name to a petition for clemency on his behalf. Even if he were truly a poet, I wouldn't have done it; but acknowledging the fact that he is not a poet and hardly a human being, I emphatically refused to assist him. While I am prepared to admit that I am neither an Egyptian nor a

Chinese expert and not able to evaluate his attempts at introducing these languages into his cantos, I am an English, Latin, and Greek scholar and I insist that in none of these tongues does Pound write poetry. He is a faker."

Graves paused for a moment, and I began to ask him about contemporary literature. "Frankly," he said, "I am pessimistic about the future prospects of literature. I don't believe that I am confronted with any sort of competition. Naturally, I believe that I am the best writer living today and I say this not out of self-adulation, but merely as a well-established fact.

"Actually, I would welcome a rush of new writers and poets, but then where shall they come from? Surely not from England, and certainly not from America. The United States, incidentally, is an odd case. It experienced some phenomenal luck in the 20's with some of its expatriate authors and it's been living on that glory ever since. Actually, American literary life is unimaginably dull and unproductive. It's amazing how a country as large and wealthy as yours should produce so painfully little."

"Were you ever in America?" I asked.

"Yes," Graves answered quickly. "I had that misfortune. I spent some time in your country not too long ago. I lectured at Princeton. It was a very interesting experience and I met some very clever and nice people, but I was never so pleased to return to Majorca in all my life. I like to read about America and I'm even pleased to meet Americans here on the island, but one thing I'm certain of, there is no single compulsion that could get me back to the States again."

"Yet," I said, "it's common knowledge on the island that there are a number of America writers that have settled around Deya and write under your tutelage."

"True," replied Graves. "But that's different. It's a very informal affair. There is no pupil-teacher relationship. Besides, we're friends. You see, I like to do what I can for young serious writers because I recall that I myself had a long, anguishing period of vacillation before my books began to earn enough money for me to live meagerly in one of the cheapest spots in Europe. In fact, it took a full fifteen years before I could in any way consider myself solvent."

My next question was directed to his personal philosophy. Instantly
he became somewhat evasive.

"I believe in the Muse of Poetry. Actually, if you want to understand more about it, I suggest that you read my book called the *White
Goddess*. You'll find it illuminating and perhaps even suggestive."

Unlike many other contemporary poets of eminence, Graves has
always been an outspoken democrat and humanitarian. "I don't like
intolerance and I despise bigotry," he said. "Some of the finest, most
sensitive Americans I've met have been Negroes. I think it's shameful
that they should be discriminated against for their color."

"Do you have any particular attitude to Jews?" I asked, knowing
beforehand that his treatment of the Jewish-Roman stuggle during
the early part of the Common Era in *Claudius, the God*, flattered the
Jews.

"My attitude to the Jews can best be summed up by stating that I
consider the Majorcans the most noble people I have ever encoun-
tered and that I am convinced that, while at least 10 per cent of them
are unmixed Marrano converts, at least 50 per cent of the rest are
predominantly of Jewish blood. I have the greatest respect for
Judaism and I have attempted to express that sentiment in my books.
It's strange though, isn't it, that the Majorcans, who are mostly Jewish
themselves and are generally free of intolerance, are strangely anti-
Semitic. Do you know that there are parts of this island where a Jew
can still not buy any land?"

"Do you believe," I asked, "that your family has fared better on
Majorca than they would have in a less primitive part of Europe?"

Graves smiled and called his youngest child to him, the boy who
had accompanied him on the beach. "This is Tomas," he said. "He is
only two and yet he already understands English and Spanish and
probably speaks Majorcan [a form of Catalonian] better than his
father. The other two children living with me are nine and thirteen.
They both speak French, Spanish, English, and Majorcan more or
less fluently and the older of the two, my daughter, has just begun on
Greek and Latin. I don't think they could learn much more in
London, do you? But, of course, there are limits. As soon as the
children reach a certain age, we send them off to boarding school in
England."

At that moment Graves's very charming wife, Beryl, entered and scowled at him and me. "Robert," she said in an irritated tone, "will you do nothing today?"

Graves seemed abashed and looked at me apologetically, almost as if to say, "Women are the bane of the world but they do see to it that the work is done."

"Just one last question," I asked hurriedly. "Do you have any plans for the future?"

"Plans?" Graves scratched his gray head. "I shall probably continue doing exactly what I have always done: writing. I expect that things might be a little easier financially for us now since I've sold the screen rights to *I, Claudius*. And I've just learned that Alec Guinness has been hired for the leading role. But that won't affect our lives very much. Majorca is very quiet, a tranquil place, and as long as I remain here I shall continue producing the best I can."-

Robert Graves Demurs

Robert Graves/1956

From *Commentary*, 22 (November 1956), 471-72.

To the Editor of Commentary:

Gratified as I am by being considered worthy of a profile in *Commentary*, I find that Mr. Arnold Sherman has made a number of misstatements which greatly embarrass me. Here are a few.

1) He did not accidentally meet me on a beach. He first came knocking at my door, without an introduction, and asked for a brief interview for a local Palma paper. I gave it to him, telling him just what to say. He printed it, and that was that. I gave him no authority to publish an interview in the U.S.

2) My only comment on American swimmers was that most of them like the water warmer than it ever gets in Britain; hence on cold days one can distinguish Americans from British.

3) I did *not* dive into the Mediterranean on the beach where we afterwards met. The water there is only about a foot deep for some twenty yards out.

4) I do *not* stack my books several feet high in my study nor do I litter the floor with magazines. I have bookshelves like everyone else, and keep things as tidy as I can.

5) The subjects of my books "range from the life of Jesus to the reign of Claudius," do they? Not a very extensive range, since the two men were close contemporaries.

6) I have brought up eight children, but only four in Majorca.

7) I do *not* translate obscure Latin treatises. Lucan's *Pharsalia* and Suetonius's *Twelve Caesars*, which will soon be on sale in the U.S.A., are neither treatises nor obscure.

8) I am *not* convinced that my poetry will endure, and never said so; and am not interested in posterity anyhow, as I have specifically recorded.

9) My remarks on Dylan Thomas, Eliot, and Pound have been

printed accurately in *The Crowning Privilege*. I repudiate Mr. Sherman's version *in toto*.

10) I do *not* claim to be a scholar in any language.

11) I do *not* believe that I am the best living writer today, and will punch anyone's nose who says either that I am, or that I claim to be.

12) I did *not* say that I had the misfortune of visiting America. I said that while in America in 1938 I lost a lot of weight and a lot of money. It was a most important experience which I would not have missed for anything.

13) There are no American writers settled in my village "who write under my tutelage" and I never said there were.

14) I never said that my *White Goddess* is "illuminating and suggestive." I never use either adjective.

15) I did *not* say more about Negroes than that I particularly liked two American Negroes who had come to Majorca: Alston Anderson the short-story writer, and Camilla Heron the anthropologist.

16) I did *not* say that there are parts of Majorca where a Jew cannot buy land. I may have said that no foreigner can buy land within five kilometers of the sea, without special permission—even Jews.

17) My children are learning Latin and French, not Greek.

18) I do *not* think that "women are the bane of the world"; but I do think amateur journalists are.

19) Alec Guinness has *not* been hired for the leading role in a screen version of my *I, Claudius*. It is not even sure whether the picture will be made.

20) I did *not* say that Majorca has no tradition of art: it has a long and magnificent one.

21) I have written about thirty books in Deyá, not ninety; ninety is the grand total.

22) I did *not* meet Ezra Pound at a dinner; I met him in Colonel T. E. Lawrence's rooms at All Souls College, Oxford. Lawrence's sensible introduction was: "Graves, Pound; Pound, Graves. You'll dislike each other."

23) I did *not* say that American literary life is "unimaginatively dull and unproductive." It is certainly far from being either.

24) My wife has never said: "Robert, will you do nothing today?" On the contrary, she is always trying to persuade me that I am

overworking. On the occasion quoted she may have foreseen, with her usual intuition, that Arnold Sherman's visit was going to do me no good in either the short or the long run. . . .

Finally, I must confess that Mr. Sherman is a nice guy and that I am sure he has not injured me on purpose; but his study of Oriental philosophy and his natural reluctance to face hard facts have combined to produce a caricature of me which, I fear, only my friends will recognize as irresponsible and absurd.

Robert Graves
Deyá, Majorca, Spain

Mr. Sherman *writes*:

Admittedly, my article was expanded from an original interview which was intended for a local Spanish newspaper but which was, to my knowledge, never published (at least not during this writer's sojourn on Majorca); if in that enlargement I have either erred or been insulting, I deeply apologize to Mr. Graves. To me it seems that my article was anything but unflattering, and certainly not insulting. . . .

Conversations with Robert Graves
John Haller/1956

From *Southwest Review,* 42 (Summer 1957), 237-41. Copyright
© 1957 by Southern Methodist University. This essay first appeared in the *Southwest Review.* Reprinted by permission.

When I decided to include a side-trip from Barcelona to Palma, in
addition to the usual return route by way of Nice, Barcelona, Madrid,
and Lisbon, I did so with the distinct hope of seeing Robert Graves. I
knew that he was somewhere in Mallorca, or had been at the time I
had last heard and, the island being a small place and he a big man, I
thought I should have no great difficulty finding him.

From the airport I went to the hotel and from the hotel straight
after my man. I went first to Fomemto de Turismo.

"I have heard of him," the attendant acknowledged, "but I do not
know the address. Why not try the police? They keep a record of all
foreign residents."

Three minutes later I stood in the inner sanctum of the Mallorcan
police force.

"Roberto Gra-ves?" repeated the official, pronouncing the name in
the Spanish fashion. "I know him, yes. The Englishman. He is here
for many years. He lives in Deyá."

Walking over to a map on a wall, he located the village and told
me how to get there. "It's a small place. Ask anyone for his house."

"Thank you very much," I said, relieved to find the problem so
quickly settled.

"Espérese!" he called, as I moved away. "He might be here in
Palma. He has a Jeep, and he shuttles back and forth with frequency."

Looking in a ledger, he located the street address and wrote it
down for me, then stepped to the door and courteously pointed out
the way.

I had no trouble finding the street and number, and after climbing
a dark stairway up to the second floor, I pressed a button on the
indicated door with keen expectancy.

A maidservant appeared. "El señor Graves?" I asked.

"Sí, señor. Síagame." She led me up more dark stairs to the third floor and rang the bell.

A large man with a large head opened the door.

"El señor Graves," said the maid, and disappeared.

"You don't know me, Mr. Graves," I said, "but I've read your books, and I came to pay my respects to the greatest living writer of English."

"Come in," he said, giving me his hand.

I picked my way across the room as best I could. Papers, books, magazines, pencils, shoes, articles of clothing, glasses, and bottles were scattered about the floor in the wildest confusion. From that room we passed to another, equally untidy. Graves took a seat and offered me another on the other side of the table. We talked discursively. I divided my attention between the man and the room, and he divided his attention between me and his twelve-year-old son to whom he was giving a Latin lesson.

I had come at a very inconvenient hour. The lesson was in full swing, and the boy could not remember how to conjugate *timere*. A younger son burst into the room bouncing a ball, a daughter suddenly appeared searching for an envelope, Mrs. Graves came in to ask for an address, and a maid opened the door to announce that dinner was ready.

"Get out, all of you!" Graves cried in sudden exasperation. "Can't you see I'm talking with a visitor? I'll be there presently."

"I'll be glad to leave," I said, getting hastily to my feet.

"No, please sit down," he insisted. "We can have a few minutes together. Where are you from?"

"Texas," I replied, with what I hoped was diffidence. "Are you surprised to find that your books are read in Texas?"

"Not particularly," he said. "I think that if I had to live in the United States, I would rather live in Texas than in any other part."

"One Englishman was there recently," I said, "and he didn't seem to like us. Of course we didn't like him either. Priestley."

"Priestley? Oh, God!"

"I don't have any use for him."

"I should hope not!"

"Did you ever hear of J. Frank Dobie?"

"No, I don't keep up well on American writers."

"I believe you would like Dobie. He's our most prominent folk-lorist."

By this time I had a chance to observe Graves well. His hair was long and unkempt, his front teeth reduced to two or three crooked and discolored stubs, his hands broad and thick. When he laughed, his mouth went up toward his nose in a peculiarly unpleasant sort of way. His dress was the extreme of slovenliness. He certainly did not look like England's greatest poet, much less like the White Goddess' chosen oracle. Yet his eyes were very expressive, and as he spoke he displayed such quickness of apprehension, such sensitivity, and such a vast range of knowledge that I felt myself about one inch high.

"I also live in Mexico part of the year," I said.

"Mexico! Of all places in the New World I should most like to visit Mexico."

"It's wonderful," I agreed. "Many Englishmen have visited there. D. H. Lawrence is the one I always think of in connection with the extraordinary *Plumed Serpent.*"

"Lawrence was a ninny," he said, "and his work unimportant." And that settled that.

"No book of recent years has impressed me as much as *The White Goddess,*" I said truthfully after a pause. "Who else can handle so much erudition with such effortless grace? The only possible comparison is Anatole France."

"Anatole France was all right in his way. Of course he wrote too much. . . . You know how I came to write *The White Goddess?* It's a very strange story." He paced restlessly up and down the room in the narrow space where the litter had been kicked to one side. "As I was working on *King Jesus* these ideas began to pop in on me one by one. Then a friend sent me this from Africa"—he showed me a curiously wrought ring—"while at the same time another friend gave me this"—he pulled out what seemed to be a very ancient coin—"and shortly afterward I found this print. All those things taken together started me on the track. . . . How much do you believe in intuition? If a writer doesn't work by intuition, what good is he?"

All this was uttered in a disjointed fashion, Graves's mind leaping from one thing to another, yet always coming back to the point of reference. All the while he continued to pace the floor, occasionally sitting down, only to jump up again almost at once.

"I've been criticized because of my allegiance to the White Goddess. After all, it's not *my* White Goddess. I'm merely her interpreter. She was here long before me. In fact, being the spirit of poetry, I should say she was rather eternal. . . . Who's your favorite American author?"

"Mark Twain," I answered unhesitatingly, bristling to his defense.

"A great man," he said quietly. "A very great man. My father met him once. He was the best."

"Have you read *The Mysterious Stranger?*" I asked. "That's the high-water mark in American literature."

"I don't recall it."

"What English authors have you known personally?" I asked. "Did you know H. G. Wells?"

"I knew Wells in his later days when he had grown very rude, opinionated, and doddering. As a younger man, however, I think he must have been quite interesting.

"I knew Hardy at first hand. He was worth knowing. Then I knew Arnold Bennett—a real man and a real gentleman. I liked Arnold very much."

"One reason I liked *The White Goddess* so much," I began after a brief pause, "is that I'm interested in trees, and your explanation of the calendar based on the successional flowering of trees fascinated me. I make my living as a tree surgeon."

"A tree surgeon!" he exclaimed. "Good heavens, I want to talk with you!"

Mrs. Graves stuck her head in to remind him that the dinner was getting cold.

"Sorry I can't ask you to lunch," he said, "but we have invited others. However, come back tomorrow if you can. Sunday we'll be in Deyá. If you're up that way, stop in."

Not wishing to return too soon, I waited until Sunday, then rented a motor-scooter and made the trip to Deyá, stopping on the way of course at Valldemosa to visit the monastery where Chopin and George Sand lived their idyllic sojourn. The cells they occupied have been converted into a museum, and among other articles for sale there was Sand's *Winter in Mallorca*, edited and translated into English for the first time by the same Robert Graves.

When I got to Deyá, I was saved the trouble of inquiring for his residence by meeting him coming along the road on foot, together with Mrs. Graves, three children, and several friends. As I slowed to a halt, he recognized me at once, introduced me to his friends, regretted that he could not have me to lunch, and insisted that I visit him in Palma on Monday at 4:00 in the afternoon.

A hundred meters farther along, I came to his house, charmingly situated among flowers and trees and commanding a magnificent view of the Mediterranean. Another hundred meters or so, and I overtook a walker with a golden beard trimmed in an unmistakably literary fashion.

"English?" I asked.

"No, American," he answered very pleasantly.

"Writer?"

"Yes."

"You know Graves, of course?"

"I'm his neighbor."

"You admire his writing, I assume?"

"His poetry very much, his prose not quite so much. But as a poet, he's tops. No argument about it."

I took leave of the golden beard and the pleasant voice and continued my trip by way of Soller, up the picturesque mountain slope with its 164 hairpin curves, and then back to Palma.

The next day at 4:00 I climbed the dark staircase and rang the bell. Again I was shown through the wilderness of books, papers, tumblers, etc., into the study proper from which the maid was just emerging.

"See what happens to my room," grumbled the great man, indicating its comparative tidiness. "I can never find anything after that woman gets through in here. . . . Have a brandy. . . . What do you know about mistletoe?"

We talked at length about that curious parasite, its growth habits propagation, occurrence, mythological significance, etc. From mistletoe we passed to trees in general. He seemed to take a special liking to me when he found that I had changed my profession from teacher of English to tree surgeon.

"Trees are not simply trees," he said. "They are something more. I think it would be hard to work with trees and remain stupid."

I had seen a lone hackberry along a street in Palma and mentioned it to him. He had never heard of a hackberry and was highly interested. (The next day I took him some leaves and fruit.) We discussed the jacaranda, the heather, the mulberry, the fig, the ebony, and others.

"The most exciting thing to come out of Mexico recently," he said, "is the mushroom oracles."

I confessed my ignorance.

"About fifteen or sixteen new varieties of mushrooms have been discovered in southern Mexico which produce visions. Hallucinations of the most fantastic kind—glittering processions of splendidly dressed figures marching along in slow and stately fashion, or seated on golden thrones. This, I think, may give us a clue to the origin of the heaven concept."

"Reminds me of peyote," I said. "The Mexican cactus consumed by the Indians to induce hallucinations."

"The mushrooms are better. No after effect."

Some people came in, and mushrooms vanished as a topic.

After introductions and small talk, Graves mentioned that he had received a letter from Anna Magnani. I had just seen her in *Suor Leticia* while in Milan and was much interested. He showed us the letter in which she accepted his invitation to play Messalina in *I, Claudius,* at the same time suggesting Alec Guinness as *il perfetto Claudio.*

After the visitors left, he told me that Irving Stone had dropped in the night before on his way to Rome, where he was to write the biography of Michelangelo.

I asked his opinion of Stone.

"A hard-working, intelligent, serious man," he said. "I was embarrassed at not having read any of his books. But I don't know why he wants to write about Michelangelo. I can't stand the man, can you?"

"He was the world's greatest," I said.

"You'd better stick to your trees."

We talked about trees again. Mrs. Graves came in and dug up a recent book on the subject which someone had sent them.

"It doesn't look like much to me," she said, derogatorily flipping through the pages.

I looked in my turn and came to a section concerned with the

mythological significance of the fig in ancient Rome. I pointed it out
to Graves, and he read a page or two suspiciously, at the same time
turning the most extraordinary shade of white.

"A silly, stupid, superficial thing!" he cried, throwing it to one side.

I bit my lip to keep from smiling at that show of professional
jealousy. Previously he had remarked that he kept no books at all
except dictionaries and standard reference works. *The Oxford English
Dictionary* stood on the shelves in all its ponderous dignity, and we
consulted it frequently during our discussion of trees. "I have to
correct it all the time," he remarked.

We argued about what wood the ark of the covenant was made
of. I thought it was *Bumelia lanuginosa,* while he claimed it was
acacia. I reminded him that "acacia" could be almost any tree with
thorns on it.

"But don't forget its derivation," he said. "*Cacos,* meaning 'bad' or
'evil,' together with the privative 'a.' The wood was one chosen to
ward off evil.

"See this," he said suddenly, picking up a polished stick curiously
enlarged and convoluted at one end. "I pulled it out of the fire. What
do you suppose made it grow that way?"

"A vine growing around it," I conjectured.

"Do you really think so? How interesting! But notice that the spiral
is counterclockwise. Do all vines grow counterclockwise?

I could not answer. He continued musing over the stick for some
minutes.

"I like to know the reason for everything," he said, "and I like
people who ask questions."

We drank some more brandy.

"How many degrees do you have?" he asked.

"Only a Master's."

"I don't have even that!" he said in triumph.

He told me he was invited to the United States to lecture on "The
Evils of Scholarship" and asked me for suggestions. That initiated a
lively discussion which lasted about an hour. We touched on
specialization, compartmentalization, university presses, educational
psychology, divinity, the ivory tower concept, and everything else we
could think of on the subject. He found pencil and paper and worked
out an outline.

"I suppose Goethe was the last of the universal genuises," I
hazarded.

"He was not a universal genius. He was a stupid old man."

Mrs. Graves came in with some tea.

"Madam, I am picking this man's brains," he explained. Then
wheeling around on me he asked, "You don't mind too much, do
you?"

"To the contrary, I'm delighted," I said. "That remark implies such
a comfortable assumption."

It was quite dark by this time. He stirred up the olive pits burning
in the brazier. I decided it was time to go and worked my way
through the litter toward the door.

"Keep in touch," he said, "and come to Deyá next Sunday if
you're still here."

"Goodbye," I said, and the impression of that large head, the
penetrating glance, and the enormous intellectual energy followed
me down the dark stairway, along the street, and into my hotel room,
so that most of the night I dreamed of Robert Graves.

Robert Graves

Huw P. Wheldon/1959

From *Monitor: An Anthology* (London: Macdonald, 1962), 88-95. Reprinted by permission.

You could be forgiven for thinking that with his Roman Emperor's face and poise, Robert Graves might show signs of imperial hauteur and a disregard for lesser mortals who had kept him waiting indefinitely, day after day, to be filmed. But our abiding memories are Graves and his wife, our filming postponed once more, fixing up breakfast for us, or lunch, or showing us the island; or, seen through the open door, Graves sitting at his desk working as if nothing was happening while his children and our confusions raged in the rest of the house. Our cameras had been impounded by the Spanish Customs authorities, and using the Graves house as our base we spent four days cabling London, telephoning Madrid, arguing with Import Licence Officials, pleading with policemen, dealing with lawyers. We might have been fighting a war. Graves remained detached, sympathetic and ironic, friendly, rather relishing the muddle, and endlessly informative about every subject under the sun.

You could also be forgiven for thinking that the author of so many works treating of history and archaeology, religion and mythology would have a large library of his own, or access to books nearby. He works, in fact, with few. He has the basic sources, Greek and Latin texts, the Bible, Josephus, the poets. He has a few encyclopaedias, any number of dictionaries, and a handful of by no means standard reference books. "All the rest are books about books. I think I have everything here that is really necessary." A few shelves in a small room hold them all.

"Prose books," he once said, "are the show dogs I breed to support my cat. . . . There's no money in poetry, but then there's no poetry in money either." He has brought up two families of four children on the proceeds of his prose. His poetry has earned him his major reputation. He draws his inspiration from the Muse—the White God-

dess—"the queen in her high silk pavilion", a personage at
once satisfyingly mystical and concrete, for she can be
incarnated "in some particular woman, who must be loved
and trusted whatever happens". It is his Muse which gives
Graves his distance from literary cliques and fashions in
poetry, for she is the person to whom he addresses himself
in his poems, in his singular and dry-toned voice.

The conversation that follows took place partly in his ten
feet by ten feet study, with Graves fingering the papers and
coins and pencils on his desk; and partly in the wild and
pretty garden, occasionally interrupted by children scorch-
ing by on scooters, or by old women coming in from the
village with fresh fish or a bundle of letters.

Wheldon: Mr. Graves, you have a great reputation for thor-
oughness, but writing so many books on so many different subjects,
don't you ever fear that you lay yourself open to the charge of being
a dilettante?

Graves: I don't object to the word dilettante any more than I
object to the word amateur. Both of them after all mean that you love
your job and I love my job. The choice is really between writing the
same book all the time as people like Erle Stanley Gardner do, or as
Trollope did, and they did it very well; it is just between that and
writing a different book every time. And that suits me, because I get
bored with the same subject and there are plenty of things to write
about, always. It is a question of working very hard and keeping
interested the whole time. If you do that, the other chap, the chap
who reads it, is not bored.

Wheldon: How many books have you written all told?

Graves: Well, I have lost count, quite honestly. About . . . When I
last counted it was something in the eighties; by now it must be a
hundred or so.

Wheldon: It is impossible to miss all these waste-paper baskets
here in this room and in other parts of the house, and it suggests that
you revise a great deal. Is that so?

Graves: Yes. When I left school I had a quarrel with my head-
master and he told me that my best friend was my waste-paper
basket. He meant it nastily, but I took it seriously. I don't mind

throwing away, because in Spain, unlike England, you get paid for
your waste-paper—about threepence a pound. I am very econom-
ical; I write on the backs of my typescript and everything goes
through a great many drafts. With prose about three or four
(*pointing*). Here is the thing I am writing at the moment, and I have
got a sequence of four stages. That's how it starts: that's how I am
breaking into the subject—and it is rather irregular; and here you see
the writing is slightly more regular to show good intentions, but the
roughing out is much the same; then it goes to be typed after which I
can see it again clearly. Then it goes through another stage here, and
later gets knocked about again, and after that it settles down. I hate
the first business of writing, but I do enjoy re-writing. It is the greatest
fun making things as easy as possible for the reader while keeping
the sense and integrity of what you are writing. I think most people
dislike re-writing. I am odd, perhaps.

Wheldon: What is the nature of this revision?

Graves: First of all I have to find out what I really mean—that I
have my facts right—then I have to find out if I have things in the
right order and when I have got the general lay-out it is a question of
minor operations for the convenience of the reader, because I have
various theories about what makes easy prose. One thing is to study
the memory length of the reader. Although one might think that
echoes die away after three or four lines, actually they persist in the
reader's mind far longer and you have to be very careful of words
ending in 'ation' or 'ition' or 'ally' or 'ative' and so on, careful not to
get them too close together, otherwise it has some effect on his mind
which worries or distracts him. It disturbs the flow. Although the
reader does not realize it himself, it is causing him difficulty. If you can
keep the sense avoiding these sound repetitions, the thing reads like
cream. Most people don't take the trouble to think about that, but I
am conscientious about my readers. . . .

Wheldon: In writing the historical books, historical reconstructions
and translations and so on that you do, I would have thought that
you would require a very big library. One of the things that has
surprised me is that you have a comparatively few books here and no
big library anywhere near you.

Graves: If you write a historical novel you don't really need many
books; you need the original histories, Latin or Greek histories,

whatever it may be. The commentaries are not necessary. There are too many commentaries. You can get drowned in commentaries. I have the histories, a lot of dictionaries and reference books and it is simply a matter of throwing myself back into the right period and living very much in that period the whole time I am writing about it. As a matter of fact, when I was writing a book called *Sergeant Lamb,* he was a Royal Welch Fusilier fighting against the Americans in the American War of Independence, my wife said: "You have laid the table for three." I had been thinking of Sargeant Lamb! It is like that. When I was writing *Claudius* there was an account of a battle he fought in Colchester with the local British king and very little information could be got from the source books, so I had to invent, and I invented. I plotted the whole battle just as I fancied it would have happened. Afterwards, I was complimented by, I think, *The Times* on having read a book which I didn't even know existed. All I had done was to trace the natural geographic way from Colchester to London—where I knew he started—and to see just where the British would have had to put their camps and what he would have done. I was very pleased when I got a large-scale map to find that the British camp was just where I expected it would be.

Wheldon: When it comes to books like *Claudius* and to classical themes generally, do you find that living by the Mediterranean is a help to you?

Graves: Oh, yes, the Mediterranean is very much the same from here right to Palestine. There is very little difference in the way of life—the same temperament, the same vegetation, the same old-fashioned ways of ploughing, pruning olives, pressing wine and so on. It doesn't require much imagination to get back. I find it a great help when I am writing these books to have some ancient evidence that these things are not stories. I like to have a coin or a piece of statue or an old tile or anything of that sort. I finger it and I think I get something out of it in an odd way. As a matter of fact, this island, Majorca, was once held by the Romans. It's all Roman country.

Wheldon: Do you feel cut off in any way by living here?

Graves: On the contrary, I feel very much centred here and I feel that the rest of the world is 'abroad' rather than the other way about. I occasionally make raids on civilization. I spend about eleven months of the year here with perhaps a fortnight in America and a fortnight in

England. I love America, but I would not like to live there—though
they roll out the red carpet rather more generously than they do in
England when I go. Here, there is no pressure at all. People are very
good to me; they are very nice people; I have been here for thirty
years.

Wheldon: When it comes to writing poetry, as against prose . . .

Graves: Oh, enormously more difficult. Poetry demands complete
privacy. I can write prose with everything going on around me. The
only thing I don't like is any tune which interferes with the rhythm in
my head of what I am reading out to myself in order to get the
rhythm right. But with poetry you have to go into a sort of . . . you
can call it a trance, if you like . . . at any rate a very deep study, and
if you are interrupted it is as fatal as being woken up just as you have
gone to sleep when you are tired out. The last poem I wrote—I don't
know if it is any good—it kept on changing its title. In the end I got it
typed and everyone was quite convinced it was the final thing, but it
proved not to be. Well, that was not a very important poem, but
really, the less important the poem, the harder you have got to work
at it to eliminate. It's a question of insulation; a poem's got to be a
sort of island in itself so that it stands up in any context. It is difficult
to read prose written three or four hundred years ago, but the poems
of Shakespeare and so on are still there—they somehow have
divorced themselves from their environment.

Wheldon: How many drafts do you find you need for a poem?

Graves: Well, it varies. Usually it takes about seven or eight: it has
gone as far as thirty-five. Usually when I get it as far as the fourth or
fifth draft I put it into typescript and then it looks different; then I can
work on it more objectively. There comes a point when I cannot take
it any further and then I put it aside for a day or two, perhaps longer,
and meanwhile my mind has been working on it without my knowing
so that I see the mistakes which I didn't realize earlier. At that point it
goes into triplicate, then I have one last look at it and either the thing
stands or else I discard it. Actually, I discard about three out of four. It
takes me a long time, very often, to decide whether the thing should
go or not.

Wheldon: How long? A year—two years?

Graves: Well, every eleven years since I was twenty-six I have
been publishing collected poems, and each time an awful lot goes;

the length of the book remains very much the same. New stuff comes in, but I find that my early selves, my middle selves and my later selves are all very fairly represented; I keep about the same amount for every period.

Wheldon: Although you have been in Majorca so long, I notice you have written very few poems about this island.

Graves: I think that England is still the land from which poems come to me. Occasionally I have put in an olive tree or something; things turn up that provoke a poem; but mainly the landscape of my poems is in England—for instance there was a cabbage-white butterfly and I wrote a poem about it called 'Flying Crooked'. It read something like this:

> *The butterfly, a cabbage-white,*
> *(His honest idiocy of flight)*
> *Will never now, it is too late,*
> *Master the art of flying straight,*
> *Yet has—who knows so well as I?—*
> *A just sense of how not to fly:*
> *He lurches here and there by guess*
> *And God and hope and hopelessness.*
> *Even the aerobatic swift*
> *Has not his flying-crooked gift.*

But that's about me—not the butterfly.

And another day I wrote a poem about some pines along by the sea where the wind had blown them back into a leaning posture. But it was not so much about the trees, as about the actual love which they represent. It is a poem called 'Lovers in the Winter' and it goes something like this:

> *The posture of the tree*
> *Shows the prevailing wind;*
> *And ours, long misery*
> *When you are long unkind.*
>
> *But forward, look, we lean—*
> *Not backward as in doubt—*
> *And still with branches green*
> *Ride our ill weather out.*

Wheldon: Do you see yourself as a writer who, as well as writing novels and essays and other works, also writes poetry, or do you regard yourself primarily as a poet?

Graves: Primarily as a poet. I made up my mind when I was fifteen years old that that would be my job, and everything I have done since has been consistent with it, apart from going into the army, which I could not very well avoid, although I was a volunteer. When I left the army, just after the First World War, I made a resolve never to be anybody's stooge. I was never going to take a job, and I have kept to that ever since. But then the question is money, one has to live. I have had two families of four children each and they take a lot of educating. That meant living by some other way. I found that writing novels and so on was a suitable way of doing it, but I have always been very careful to avoid getting mixed up with any political party or church or club—I belong to no organization at all because I feel that a poet should be completely independent and able to do what he wants in his own way.

Wheldon: So that as a poet you are totally committed to something?

Graves: I am totally committed to poetry, and if you ask me what poetry means I should give you a million answers. But I think of poetic truth, which is what I am trying to get, as quite distinct from historic truth or scientific truth or any sort of rational truth. It is a sort of supra-rational truth.

Wheldon: Is it distinct from religious truth?

Graves: Well, you have to distinguish when you talk about religious truth, whether you mean real religion or whether you mean church religion—ecclesiastical religion. I think it comes very close to the natural faith of religion. But a great many poets have confused it with music or philosophy or rhetoric, or have gone astray in that way.

Wheldon: What poets have gone astray?

Graves: Oh, there have been a great many of them. I should say Milton went astray when he accepted a job from Cromwell's people as a secretary to the Council of State. Wordsworth went astray when he accepted a sinecure as a distributor of stamps in Westmorland. It shows in their poems.

Wheldon: Is it still going astray if you just take a job in, say, a post office?

Graves: It depends entirely how much you are committed to your job. You can be an anonymous post office clerk and that is all right. But as soon as you have to identify yourself with the Postmaster General's office you are sunk, I should say, as a poet.

Wheldon: A lot of obscure poetry is written, but your poetry seems to me particularly clear. Yet, you have said that, as a poet your poetry is not written for the public.

Graves: It is written for the sake of the poem itself. The public, when you write a poem, is like the little figure you put in an architectural drawing that shows the scale. You are not addressing that person.

Wheldon: Are you then addressing yourself?

Graves: No, I suppose I am just doing a little bit of magic. I am putting a ring round a piece of experience so that it can stay, and anybody is welcome to find it who understands poetry. It may last, it may not. That is not my concern. I have done my best to insulate it against what is not poetry.

Wheldon: And if it is a true poem it will go on persisting for a long time?

Graves: Oh, a poem that can walk off the page and run away, you can never catch.

Wheldon: A lot of your poetry seems to me, despite the fact that it is written in lovely surroundings, to be very troubled poetry. Is that right?

Graves: Yes, poetry to me rather means trouble. I remember once, when I was a very young man and Thomas Hardy was a very old man, I was staying with him down in Dorchester, and he said to me, "You know, the critics say that I'm a pessimist." And I said, "Well, are you, Mr. Hardy?" And he said, "I took the trouble to go through my poems the other day with a pencil and paper, marking each one of them with one of three marks, a 'U' for unhappy, an 'H' for happy, and an 'N' for neutral. And," he said, "I found that they really evened out rather well." I think that if you went through my poems you would find about the same proportion, although I think the troubled ones are rather more interesting.

A *Redbook* Dialogue

Gina Lollobrigida/1963

From *Redbook,* 121 (September 1963), 112, 114-15, 117.

When the noted English author and poet Robert Graves agreed to participate in a *Redbook* Dialogue, he made only one stipulation: no academicians, no writers. Actress Gina Lollobrigida, equally delighted to talk with someone far removed from her own profession, met Mr. Graves in New York City for the following conversation, which both were reluctant to bring to an end.

Robert Graves: Gina, have you got—this is a funny question—have you a secret garden to which you can retreat in your mind?

    Gina Lollobrigida: (*hesitantly*): A secret garden?

    Mr. Graves: Yes, an imaginary place—a sort of living heaven of your own in your mind, where you can go to be alone. (*After a pause*) *Un jardin imaginaire?*

    Miss Lollobrigida: No.

    Mr. Graves: I daresay you had it once. When you were young you probably had an imaginary paradise. Many young girls do. But later it's lost. Perhaps now you no longer need a place to which you can retreat. The nature of the acting profession does accustom you to being surrounded by people, must even make you want to have them around just because there's so much going on.

    Miss Lollobrigida: No I—for the work I do: I have to be with so many people. But I feel sometimes more alone in a lot of people than when I'm completely alone.

    Mr. Graves: Yes, yes.

    Miss Lollobrigida: And I—some years ago, people had a kind of obsession to look at me and so I did not have the normal life as I had before. There was all this admiration, people always looking at me. It gave me some problems, really. I kept having this nightmare. I dreamed to be in a bed without clothes on and people staring at me. Was something dreadful.

Mr. Graves: Horrible.

Miss Lollobrigida: And that's because of—you know . . .

Mr. Graves: I would say that's because there are so many people who think of you in that way. It must be horrible.

Miss Lollobrigida: For that reason, I don't understand how the people in my business—actresses—I don't understand how they can enjoy success. How can they proud of that, to be watched all the time?

Mr. Graves: But, Gina, people are so accustomed to looking at women on the screen merely as sex symbols that they make the mistake of thinking that you are one. And you're fighting it the whole time.

Miss Lollobrigida: (*almost inaudibly*) Yes.

Mr. Graves: I must tell you, Gina, that I was *bouleverse*—most overcome that you agreed to be my . . . interlocutrix, I think the word is on this occasion. Because I live away from things and seldom go to the cinema and yet somehow get a sense of who's what in the motion picture industry. I get an understanding of what different actresses represent to the public. While I don't want to be scandalous and mention names of those who are there to rouse merely lascivious interest or perhaps sickly sentimentality, from the start I've been conscious that you are communicating something quite different— call it the goodness and truth of woman.

Miss Lollobrigida: I've received a really beautiful compliment.

Mr. Graves: It's not my job to pay compliments. What I mean is that in spite of all dirty work by producers and script writers to spoil things, you still show that the public image is not necessarily fraudulent or obscene. And I have never met anybody off the screen who didn't correspond with my impression of them on the screen.

Miss Lollobrigida: You mean that actresses, even when they are playing parts, they are themselves anyway?

Mr. Graves: I mean that in spite of all the tricks of the camera, actors and actresses can't deceive a person who feels through his finger tips . . . If you see what I mean. My friend Alec Guiness, for example: he always remains himself in spite of the terrible parts he has to play sometimes. We were talking about this one day and I

said, "Look, Alex—look at your handwriting. With handwriting like
that, you're all right whatever character you have to play—firm,
splendid, optimistic." And you know that you can trust a man like
that. Tell me, Gina, how many real people do you know, present
company excepted? How many real people, absolutely real?

Miss Lollobrigida: Very, very few.

Mr. Graves: I'm lucky. I know about twenty. All my life I've been
sort of picking these people up and sorting them out and being aware
of their existence, and it's very, very strange each time you recognize
that So and So has this quality which you can't define. The more
you talk about it, the less it means. It's a recognition of a certain
quality which can perform miracles. (*Miss Lollabrigida nods.*) You
understand—we need say no more.

Miss Lollobrigida: Yes.

Mr. Graves: Every now and then you meet it and it makes you
feel splendid. It is one of the few joys in this world to recognize that
quality.

Miss Lollobrigida: Is in a way to have real friends. Is that what
you mean?

Mr. Graves: They become your friends, and so much that if they
said to you, "Fly to the North Pole tomorrow because I need you
there," then you'd go. And you'd know that it wasn't for any wrong
reason.

Miss Lollobrigida: And it's funny how a friend relationship can
last longer than love.

Mr. Graves: But it is a form of love. It's different from physical
love.

Miss Lollobrigida: Yes, but it lasts longer.

Mr. Graves: It can last longer if you're unlucky in love. But you
know, Gina . . .

Miss Lollobrigida: I think that love between a man and a
woman is physical love. But a friend relationship, it's a different kind
of love.

Mr. Graves: The interesting thing is when you find in your own
children that particular quality—this integrity, this realness that we've
been talking about. You don't expect to find it in your own children,
and when you do, it's scary. But then, there are no rules. It can
emerge in anyone, completely unpredictable. And this fact makes the

world so alive. If it wasn't for the few real people, all this (*gesturing to include the whole world*) would slide into the sea.

Miss Lollobrigida: Your children are lucky to have a good example.

Mr. Graves: A good mother.

Miss Lollobrigida: Yes, I am sure. And your children see you working at home?

Mr. Graves: Yes, but I don't think they ever paid much attention to what I was doing. When they went to school, though, they were asked: "Are you any relation to Robert Graves?" and then if they did badly in their English papers and so on, they were bullied by the masters, who would scold them by saying, "Your father would be ashamed of you." My children never realized, you see, that I was a well-known writer. I mean, we just live in a sort of healthy home in Majorca. Now, of course, they're more or less resigned to it.

Miss Lollobrigida: They keep the house quiet when you write.

Mr. Graves: They don't treat my study as sacred. I have no special hours, and if I'm interrupted, I'm interrupted. That's just too bad. I teach the youngest boy Latin and Scripture and help the elder girl with her Latin, and so on. I've had eight children, you see. One was killed in the last war, and there's thirty-four years between the eldest and the youngest. (*After a moment*) And none of them reads books.

Miss Lollobrigida: No?

Mr. Graves: No. And why should they? We live in Spain, where people don't read books. But my son William, he's an oil geologist in the Sahara, where you have nothing to do all day—he has recently started educating himself.

Miss Lollobrigida: But you didn't push them to—

Mr. Graves: No. Why should I? They hear a lot of talk which goes on—we have any amount of people coming to us, intellectuals, nonintellectuals, actors, doctors, painters, musicians, all sorts of odd people with whom I have some kind of connection—and the children hear us talking and pick up alot. But they—the idea of doing the same job as me would not occur to them. Because I think one always wants to break off from tradition. Another son of mine, for example, is an architect.

Miss Lollobrigida: I thought that just as the . . . (*After a long* *pause*) My dream for my son is that he will be far away from movie business.

Mr. Graves: All movie mothers say that.

Miss Lollobrigida: No, but for a father that is a writer, a genius— I think it's the opposite. Should be nurtured, to have sons that continue writing.

Mr. Graves: Well, you can't regulate that. My father was a writer, and his father was a writer, and his father was a writer—

Miss Lollobrigida: So they will break the rules, your sons?

Mr. Graves: My father tried to stop me being a writer. He wanted me to be a schoolmaster. Besides, I had to starve for about twelve years before I could ever make a living as a writer. I'm eccentric, in a way. I suppose I'm the last writer who writes on scores of different subjects and doesn't corner the market but just feels he *has* to write for a particular book and then anybody who wishes to publish it, can. The whole trend in publishing is to suppress that sort of freedom and make everybody specialize. But I've always—I've written prose books in order to afford writing poetry, and I say somewhere that it's like breeding dogs because you have a favorite cat and want to give it milk.

Miss Lollobrigida: Is too bad that today people do not read much poetry.

Mr. Graves: And do you know why?

Miss Lollobrigida: No.

Mr. Graves: Because the poets aren't doing their job. Poetry has become a matter of literary fashion and keeping up with the avant-garde. But the only poetry that has any use is poetry with a particular magic which comes to the poet by reflection from his muse. Now, the word "muse" has been abused down the centuries but it has a very important connotation—the idea of a relation between a man and a woman which cuts across all societal boundaries of class or religion or even matrimony. There is a recognition in a man and woman of a love which depends on wisdom. The wisdom comes from the woman and is reflected onto the man and he incorporates that in his poetry. Poets have got to be men to deserve muses.

Miss Lollobrigida: (*shaking her head*) That is something not easy to find these days, a man who is a man.

Mr. Graves: I agree. I have lectured at colleges here, you know, and I see all these beautiful girls—they're intelligent, they're lovely, they're so, well, *soignée,* beautiful stockings—and their escorts are waiting for them, dirty, scruffy, talking only about ball games . . . you know loutish. And to think that these beautiful girls should have such terrible choice of husbands! Sad. But there are just more good women about than there are good men.

Miss Lollobrigida: Even when they have to give me a partner for a film they say, "At least he is a man!" You know! "He's a *man!*" They don't say to me, "He's a good actor." They say that I must be happy to have a man!

Mr. Graves: Well, that's what's wrong with poetry nowadays. So few poets are men, and a great many are pretending to be women.

Miss Lollobrigida: You might say that it's the fault of the women, but I don't blame them.

Mr. Graves: Oh, no, it's not the fault of the women. It's the fault of the—

Miss Lollobrigida: Of the women being stronger so the men feel weak?

Mr. Graves: No, it's—it has something to do with the lack of any real controlling element in modern life. Money is the only thing that has become a god in its own right. Religion in the United States— there are small local exceptions where religion means something, but basically all religious strength has gone, and all you can do is admit money as the god, and the ritual is buying and selling. And a lot of people behave very well in this particular worship of money. But it's not enough.

Miss Lollobrigida: Why is the money so important?

Mr. Graves: Because love has gone. Love and honor. They are the two great things, and now they're dimmed and blighted. Today love is just sex or sentimentality. Love is really a recognition of truth, a recognition of another person's integrity and truth in a way that is compatible with—that makes both of you light up when you recognize that quality in the other. That's what love is. It's a recognition of singularity, I should say. And love is giving and giving and giving.

Miss Lollobrigida: Yes. Is generosity.

Mr. Graves: And is not looking for any return. Until you do that, you can't love.

Miss Lollobrigida: This is true. I *believe* that. But in America, the talk is all the time about sex. I think it's a kind of obsession. Everything is sex or not sex.

Mr. Graves: That's all they have to think about, except money.

Miss Lollobrigida: It's funny, though, the talk isn't the same as the doing. In the United States, you can walk on the street and nothing happens, not like in Italy. The women, they can't go alone anywhere, otherwise they have some trouble with men. The Italian man, he sees a woman alone on the street and immediately he feels like a male, and instead of thinking silent what he feels, he wants to show his masculinity in saying strong things—but loud, you know, like on a stage. What happens to me is terrible. They talk about me as if they were in another room, and they say everything they want to say, and for a woman to stand there and hear such things and not to answer back to them, it's terrible.

Mr. Graves: (*reassuringly*) Never mind. You'll survive.

Miss Lollobrigida: (*with a quick smile*): Yes.

Mr. Graves: Of course. It is much more difficult for you to keep your public image separate from your private life than it is for me. I should imagine it causes some difficulty for your family.

Miss Lollobrigida: I think my son is not—he does not understand yet what I'm doing, the fact that I'm popular. He is just six years old. I just wonder what will be the reaction one day when he will find out that his mother is a—

Mr. Graves: (*teasing*) Is a what?

Miss Lollobrigida: . . . is a star. He was frightened when the people were too much, in Canada, and then he was jealous that all the people would call me Gina and so suddenly he started to call me Gina too.

Mr. Graves: Well, why not?

Miss Lollobrigida: And just lately he asked me, "But why, Mommy, they ask you to write your name on a paper?" And I didn't know what to say. Then I think he finds the answer himself, and he said, "Oh, I know, they want a souvenir."

Mr. Graves: He thinks for himself?

Miss Lollobrigida: Yes, yes. I came back from Paris one day, and the chauffeur came with little Milko, "What did you do?" He was ashamed to tell me and it took a long time to get the truth. Because he has so much fantasy, my son, and so he was telling me other stories but not the real one. So I said, "Look, Milko, you must tell me because anyhow I know." So he said, "How do you know? You were in Paris. You can't know." I said, "Yes, I know. The Holy Ghost told me, and He knows everything." Then finally he realized that he had to say the truth, so he said he tied the little girl to a chair and then hit her on the tummy because he was a crocodile.

The day after, when Milko came back from school, I asked him what he had done in school. So he said to me, "Why don't you ask the Holy Ghost?"

Mr. Graves: Absolutely right.

Miss Lollobrigida: The first years, there was much trouble with my baby. For instance, when I was in Spain, I was doing *Solomon and Sheba,* and I had long hair, long dress, funny make-up, so Milko didn't recognize me and he was scared.

Mr. Graves: Yes, I can see that. And one thing you've not been able to give him is a fixed home. He's always going from one place to another.

Miss Lollobrigida: But that was less important than my face. I remember even when he was in love with his nurse—of course, I was jealous of the nurse because he was more affectionate to her than to me—but even her, when she had the day free and she changed the white dress that she had every day, he didn't like her. And with me, you know, it was my first child and I was suffering sometimes. I was always putting my make-up on early in the morning, six o'clock, and when the baby woke up, he saw me always with a half face black, half face white, so he cried, and didn't want to come to me or kiss me. So I took my child and then (*laughing, speaking with mock severity*) I said, "You are my son—you must love me!" So he was even more scared. Now is a little better because he understands it is just the work I do.

Mr. Graves: When I spoke of having one place to live, I was thinking of my own children. They have a stable home and a geographical center and they know all the people in the village. Although they speak English, they prefer our local language, which is Majorcan. And they have a sort of mystique about their home that gives them a strength which I'm very sorry your son has been denied. He'll make do, I'm sure, judging from your account, but it is a great help to most children to have a place of their own, a home.

Miss Lollobrigida: Is different now because he will start to go to school and will be in one place and stay there. And I will go to him; he will not travel with me.

Mr. Graves: Good.

Miss Lollobrigida: He speaks Italian, English and French already, so I asked him what he wanted to study, and he said Italian. I'm glad he chose Italian, but anyhow I would make him study it because at least then I can speak with him. Already he knows English better than me. Sometimes I have to ask him, "What are you talking about? What is this?" So he makes the translation. I would like to know the language perfect because when I read a book now I lose a lot.

Mr. Graves: Well, most books are so badly written it's not your fault.

Miss Lollobrigida: (*with a smile*): No—

Mr. Graves: It is so. Most writing is bad, bad, bad, and entirely inconsiderate of the reader.

Miss Lollobrigida: What is difficult in English is that the people, they don't talk—they don't speak as they write.

Mr. Graves: No, they don't.

Miss Lollobrigida: I mean, if you read an Italian paper or an Italian book, the people, they talk as they write. In English is not so. Even it happens sometimes when I try to read a paper and I go to the dictionary and I cannot find the words. Is a very strange language, the English.

Mr. Graves: Yes, and there are two languages. There is the spoken language and the written language. If you make a marvelous speech, one that throws the audience into a trance, you know, you write it down and it makes nonsense as writing. I don't claim to be able to entrance an audience myself; all the same I never publish any of my speeches directly. I've got to rewrite every page four times before I get it into ordinary reading shape. So it's not your fault, Gina.

Miss Lollobrigida: So English writing is complicated.

Mr. Graves: It's very complicated. And very few people take any trouble about it because they do it on typewriters, and then at least it *looks* all right because it's typed. (*Miss Lollobrigida laughs delight-edly*), but real writers never use the typewriter.

Miss Lollobrigida: I think is all so complicated, the English writing, because the English language is so rich.

Mr. Graves: Impossibly rich. You've got to live with English the whole time, and read and read, and always consult dictionaries which give the history of words, and go on learning all the time. I'm just beginning to know a little about English after working for fifty years.

Miss Lollobrigida: So what about me?

Mr. Graves: Well, don't try, my dear.

Miss Lollobrigida: I let my son be my translator, yes?

Mr. Graves: Does he hear much English spoken?

Miss Lollobrigida: He likes stories and we have read to him. And he knows—oh la la!—he remembers . . . he has a fantastic memory. Not like me. We read two, three times the same books because he likes to. But sometimes I don't pronounce well the English, so immediately Milko says, "No, is not so." And he corrects me because he remembers.

Mr. Graves: I must send him some of my children's books. I've written three recently. One's called *The Big Green Book.*

Miss Lollobrigida: Yes, I heard about that. I'm so glad. What is the story?

Mr. Graves: Oh, about a little boy who learned some magical skills from an old book and used them to tease his uncle and aunt. A child's mind is simple yet complicated.

Miss Lollobrigida: They like to know the world and everything as quickly as possible. That's why they like stories. My son likes always real stories, and the stories I tell him must be the story of Mommy and Milko, not fantasy things.

Mr. Graves: Yes. They've got to be able to identify themselves with the story. And then there are certain magical things which happen in a childhood, extraordinary experiences that children have which one remembers and can put into their stories for them. My father, who was a poet and a songwriter, used to tell us stories, and he always started in the same phrase. He said, "And so the old gardener took out his red pocket handkerchief and blew his nose." That was a sort of spell to make us accept the story. Once he started like that it was better than "once upon a time."

Miss Lollobrigida: My son, he wants always "Once upon a time." If I don't start the story like that, he doesn't like it.

Mr. Graves: Well, you can borrow my father's phrase, if you like. And I would like to give you something as a present—this poem which I wrote the other night.

Miss Lollobrigida: *(delightedly)*: Thank you. Thank you . . . Will you read it?

Mr. Graves: It's called "Not to Sleep" *(reading)*:

Not to sleep all the night long, for pure joy
Counting no sheep and careless of chimes,
Welcoming the dawn confabulation
Of birds, her children, who discuss idly
Fanciful details of the promised coming—
Will she be wearing red, or russet, or blue,
Or pure white?—whatever she wears, glorious;
Not to sleep all the night long, for pure joy,
This is given to few but at last to me.
So that when I laugh and stretch and leap from bed
I shall glide downstairs, my feet brushing the carpet
In a courtesy to civilized progression.
Though, did I wish, I could soar through the open window
And perch on a branch above, acceptable ally
Of the birds, still alert, grumbling gently together.

Miss Lollobrigida: Is lovely.

Mr. Graves: That's what it's like to be in love and happy.

Miss Lollobrigida: All this will be a beautiful souvenier, as my little Milko says.

The Poet and the Peasant

Kenneth Allsop/1965

From *Scan* (London: Hodder and Stoughton, 1965), 29-33.
Reprinted with permission.

"After a lifetime of relative anonymity, it is astonishing to find everybody rolling out the red carpet for one," says Robert Graves, briefly in Britain from his Majorca domicile.

Anonymity does not appear to be the most striking characteristic of the burly six-foot two-inch poet and novelist with the rumpled grey curls, craggy nose and full lips of a Roman caesar, and attired in pink silk tie, silver-buttoned striped waistcoat, and tan lightweight suit of American collegiate style.

Esteem was expressed through the awards of the Hawthornden, James Tait Black, Femina Vie Heureuse, Poetry Society of America and William Foyle Poetry prizes, but anonymity in the sense of absence of popular success was largely the result of his impatient indifference to the rules of literarymanship. For Robert Graves is one of the last survivors of the bohemian Mediterranean colonists of the 'Twenties, the expatriate generation of D. H. Lawrence, Gertrude Stein and Norman Douglas.

Others nomadically came and went, but Mr. Graves stayed put in the distant sun, writing to his own taste and turn of mind, and in the process producing some of the most important and original English poetry of this century, a strength and consistency apparent in the forty-five years spanned by his *Collected Poems*.

"Of course money was often hideously short," continues Mr. Graves, puffing Gauloise in short, furious spurts, padding like a training boxer (he did box and broke that heroic nose playing Rugby) up and down the Maida Vale flat. "Four years ago my total assets were 100 dollars in America and £7 in Britain. But that's never been a thing that's bothered me much. One can always make money if one wants to. The joke will be if too much money rains into my pockets—how shall I be able to stop the flow? How shall I avoid buying an ocean yacht?

"The fact is, I've no gift for luxurious living. This suit is ten years old. I've had my overcoat for twenty-eight years. The best part of living on Majorca is that I don't have to belong to any clubs or keep up with the Gonzaleses. I took this decision a long time ago. I decided after the First World War that I was never again going to be anybody's stooge."

Born in Wimbledon of mixed Irish and German blood, Mr. Graves attended Charterhouse and fought on the Western Front where he was so severely wounded that his parents were notified of his death. Married and with the first of his eight children, he ran a shop to support himself at Oxford.

In 1929 he wrote his bitter denunciation of the war, the famous *Goodbye To All That*, and went off to settle on five rocky Majorcan acres. Since then he has published 120 books, including Biblical studies and classical translations that have sold hugely in paperback editions but aroused the ire of pedant scholars. Their blood has been most curdled by his translation of Homer's *Iliad* which blows a gust of laughter through the stagnant reverence in which it was pickled for use as a schoolroom textbook.

Although it is more than fifty years since he was at Charterhouse being tortured by Homer—driven near to Homercide—he decided that this should be put up with no longer, so produced his personal revision and translation of the *Iliad*, *The Anger of Achilles*.

Mr. Graves takes the view that for 2,600 years Homer has been done wrong—in both senses. The *Iliad* has been ill-treated. For centuries purists and classicists have buried the real meaning deeper under the dust of their own platitudes; the verse has been pickled in prosiness. The point missed by dreary generations of dull dogs, says Mr. Graves, is Homer's caustic humour.

"Homer," states Mr. Graves, "was an entertainer; he had to earn a living; he knew that humour was what the public wanted. His pictures of the king-gods of his day—who had ceased to be divine—were all caricatures. His whole attitude to the gods is pure comedy—but what I like about the chap is that he was at bottom a religious man.

"For political reasons Peisistratus took up the *Iliad*, dubbed in lines and turned it into a sacrosanct epic that would give Athens status, and Homer became the basis of all education. It is that solemn atmosphere that has prevailed.

"What has been missed is that Homer's jokes were all deadpan. He delighted in guying terrible old bores. He had the comic dignity of the old Irish and Welsh story-tellers, and he wrapped up his jokes in archaic language—not his contemporary language at all.

"He had to keep a very straight face and conceal his dirty cracks to avoid libel. He was like Cervantes, no more serious and as serious, cynical but a man of deep human sympathy.

"I don't care if this translation has shocked scholars. I care about Homer—and he has been misrepresented for centuries."

Yet Mr. Graves admits some embarrassment:

"When a Greek scholar asks me what I've been working on, I mumble, 'A translation of the *Iliad*.' He then says, 'Oh, but aren't there dozens on the market! What sort of Classical degree did you get at Oxford?' And I, mumbling even more, confess, 'Well, actually, I switched from Classics to English, and didn't sit for my finals.'

"All I wanted to do was demonstrate that Homer wasn't a solemn old windbag, but an iconoclast with a deep sense of irony who had to wrap up his jokes about the gods and his lampooning of the ancient heroes to get them by his stuffy public.

"He wrote satire, not pompous tragedy, an attitude that has been consistently misunderstood. The *Iliad* has been murdered by generations of schoolmasters who've treated it either with exaggerated reverence—or with no reverence at all, but as a corpse for dramatic dissection."

Certainly, Mr. Graves's clear, lyrical prose stripped the stale fustian from Homer as most have known him, and revealed his characters in a new light.

Zeus is a boaster, full of ballyhoo and hot air, who makes himself look pretty silly with his empty vainglory. Hera is a shrew, mean and malicious, whose only virtue is her suburban morality. Athene is a spoilt brat, an ancient world Beauty Queen type. Priam's nine sons are idle and trivial playboys. Ares is a stupid lout. Agamemnon, for so long enshrined as the war-lord of the Acheans, is a ham-handed, jingoistic clown.

Homer's implicit attitude in his stories, Mr. Graves disclosed, was a loathing of war, an agnostic impatience with the superstitions, then still held, that the deities had power of intervention in human affairs. As his audiences were crass, snobbish princelings of the most reactionary and anti-intellectual breed, he could not openly scorn either the conventions or the Olympians. Instead he subtly salted his epics with caricatures of the king-gods and cartoons of battles.

In fact, so fundamentally contemptuous of the stupidities of war was he, that he barely bothered to get his military background accurate. His fighting is a careless muddle (which may justify the instinctive feeling of many a young pupil about this), and he indiscriminately mixed up modern and outmoded weapons and tactics.

"To earn his slices of fat roast mutton and his cup of honey-sweet wine at court," Mr. Graves explains, "Homer often had to strain his imagination in describing novel varieties of manslaughter, which he credited to the ancestors of his hosts."

At sixty-eight, Mr. Graves maintains a frequency of publication which has evoked the suggestion that a Graves-of-the Month Club should be started. He has given his reason for such industry as: "Eight children." Yet when he decamped to Majorca it was to find "the independence for pursuing a secret vice: poetry.

"Prose has been my livelihood, but I have used it to sharpen my sense of the altogether different nature of poetry. Prose books are the show dogs I breed and sell to support my cat."

Mr. Graves recalls without drama or horror his recent time of near-bankruptcy—"My own fault for spending years at a time on books that could never possibly cover overheads. There's no money in poetry, but, then, there's no poetry in money, either."

Nor does the sudden access of acclaim and financial success (including 30,000 dollars for his manuscripts from Buffalo University) impress him deeply.

"It happens, you know," he continues. "A kind of law operates—a vacuum occurs and someone is pushed up to fill it. It seems to be my turn."

I remind him of his lines expressing nausea at becoming a public monument:

And the punishment is fixed . . .
To be cast in bronze for a city square,
To dribble green in times of rain . . .

Did he, I ask, now feel menaced by homage?

"No danger of that," he replies. "Ten months of the year I'm living my peasant existence in Majorca with no public to put up monuments.

"I haven't changed my way of writing or way of life in the past forty years, and shan't now. Simply that the time comes when people begin to take notice. It makes no difference at all. It may embarrass my children, but not me!"

That same austere indifference to outward vogues and *vagues* has forged his powerful, spare poetry that, pre-war, seemed too untormented, lucid and a-political to be of its time.

And, although drolly scathing about his own literary standing, Mr. Graves has been equally scathing about that of other poets, dead and alive. On Pope: "A sedulous ape." On Shelley: "Voice is too shrill." On Wordsworth: "He disowned and betrayed his Muse." On Pound: "Cloacinal ranting, snook-cocking, psuedo-professional jargon."

On Dylan Thomas: "He gave his radio audience what they wanted." On Eliot: "His poetic heart has died and been given a separate funeral, but he continues to visit the grave wistfully and lay flowers on it."

And on Auden, Oxford's previous Professor of Poetry: "The prescribed period style of the 'Fifties—compounds of all the personal styles available."

He does not conceal his gratification that now, after many changes in the theory of poetry's function, his own belief is heeded, that good poetry must in essence be concerned with "the single grand theme—man's birth through woman, his love and death in the arms of a woman, which most modern poets have forgotten".

During his Oxford residence he found undergraduates "very much in agreement with my view that the old ornate Victorian tradition is completely broken and the succeeding Franco-American modernism is bankrupt.

"I saw hope on a return to the understanding that the heart-core of English poetry is inspiration from one's Muse—the judge and keeper of one's conscience, one's vision of personal truth—and not slick rhetoric, not smart contemporariness, not self-pity, and not deliberately difficult highbrowism.

"The magic that a poem can have can come only from one's Muse."

Robert Graves at Home

Frank Kersnowski/1969

Excerpts from Robert Graves's letters are published with the permission of Beryl Graves.

Even though Robert Graves had agreed to my visiting him at his home in Deyá, actually seeing him was difficult. I don't mean physically since he lived a short distance from the small hotel run by his son William, where I stayed, but mentally. What would I say to the man whose life and writings embodied much that I believed?

William laughed when I suggested that I phone first: "Robert doesn't have a phone. Just walk down to the house." I did and was asked to go into his study.

"You're busy. I'll come back another time."

"No, no. Come in. Anyone who has anything to say is always welcome."

So Robert Graves invited me in, where I sat on the sea chest. He came from behind his desk to shake my hand. On the wall to his right were shelved reference books, to his left a wall of books by and about him. The Persian saddlebags covering the chest gave me a chance to speak, to say something of their origin: north towards the Urals. Thus the conversation turned to the rug under his desk:

"Do you know who sheared the sheep, spun the wool, wove the rug?" It was not really a question. "Ben Gurion," he added.

As he spoke and continued revising the poem on his desk, he revealed a self I had expected, that of a man who by myth and magic simplified the ordinary complexities of life into the timeless exultations and complaints of the eternally youthful lover. Since at least 1949, Graves had held fast to the revelation of "To Juan at the Winter Solstice": "There is one story and one story only / That will prove worth your telling. . . ." For Graves, the story is about the rule of the goddess. Unquestioningly Graves insists that all right-feeling people will follow his lead. He has remained the ever young singer of love.

He revised the poem before him as we talked. He worked with pen on a typed page, and beside him was a stack of perhaps twenty sheets, which he told me had been four times as large before he began "the joy of writing," as he called revising. This involved act of revision seems contradictory to his need of inspiration from the muse. The finished poems, however, have immediacy and spontaneity equal to that sought after by Italian sonneteers in the Renaissance, and probably achieved with efforts no less than Graves's. As Albert Lord, who wrote *Singer of Tales*, once told me, some explanation of the values of inspiration and revision for the poet lies in the fact that the poem "in the written tradition is complete when it is published, but the poem in the oral tradition is complete when it is performed."

Graves's poem revised and copied out in ink, he handed it to me, asking, "What do you think?" The question's difficulty obliterated any possibility of rational response; and after reading a poem castigating a homosexual who made his choice because he disliked women, not because he liked men, I unthinkingly said,

"It's horrible."

"Yes. That's the word, *horrible*. It is 'horrible.' " Graves's record of such castigations of men is long.

Since my visit I have learned that others also had Robert Graves show them the items arranged on shelves in his study. But no one found the experience more unforgettable than I. As he showed me each item, he would ask, "Do you know what this is?" And for each item, my answer was unfailingly negative.

"This stone was given me by a friend who found it in a shop and bought it because it reminded him of me. When I was at Oxford recently, I asked a scholar of Arabic languages to translate the message carved on it for me. He refused, saying it was all about Robert Graves and very personal."

"Experiences like that are unforgetable."

"You've had them?"

"Yes."

"Then you understand."

Then there was the curved dagger in a worked silver scabbard:

"There are only thirty-three of these in the world. And only the sons of prophet have them. That's why I have this one."

The morning passed and lunchtime approached. I rose to leave, then found myself staying for lunch and pleased that the salad dressing I helped Robert make found favor. Another time, I helped him with preserves. That day, his wife Beryl met me at the kitchen door as Robert, wearing a blue cambry shirt and a red bandana, pared fruit. He looked up and said to come in, and when I commented that I had often helped my grandmother make jellies and preserves, he responded, "Your granny never made preserves like these!" True, but neither had he ever had my granny's damson preserves.

Later we walked to the village to get the mail and talked of words and their lives, of myths and of the spirit.

"Do you think of yourself as Slavic?"

"Not until recently. I was, quite honestly, surprised to find that I am Slavic."

"Yes. It can happen that way. And once you know about it, it becomes very important." He talked openly of his life as we walked:

"I was a virgin until I was married. And slept with no other woman until my wife forced me to. I left with that woman, and my wife left with her husband." Having only the usual academic gossip about Graves and Laura Riding and remembering that in the last paragraph of the last chapter of the revised version of *Goodbye To All That* Graves designated such stories as "unpublishable," I was surprised by his openness. A mutual friend explained. Larry Wallrich, a publisher and book dealer, had known Graves in Mallorca and kept in touch with him: "Robert's a village dweller. He has no secrets."

But our conversation could not long stay with the past. This was late in the summer of 1969, and men had just walked on the moon for the first time. That act, Robert said, was "the greatest crime against humanity in two thousand years, though being an American you may not think so." Alexander's cutting the Ghordian knot was the earlier offense to tradition. Graves believed deeply that it was Alexander's defiance of ancient custom that brought ruin on Greek civilization. Later I asked him more about his linking the two innovative acts, and on 25 February 1972 he responded:

"Yes, that 'crime against humanity.' It is being paid for already, & will be their ruin." Time for Graves seems marked by the distance culture had moved away from the early matriarchy he believed in without question, a distance divided into epochs it seems by masculine error. For Graves the mechanistic (masculine) standardization of human behavior departed from the natural order by substituting the worship of rationality for worship of the goddess. What he regarded as the concomitant confusion of sex roles he found equally unacceptable, as he made clear in a letter to me dated 18 February 1970: "My only regret about the Woman's Liberation Front is that it is an *organization* rather than a natural spread of ideas. Organizations are male in origin and procedure; and get infiltrated."

Though I helped Robert Graves make salad dressing and preserves, I did not think that his concern with housekeeping extended to such complex organizing as would be necessary in a household encompassing husband and wife, children and grand-children, muses of various tenures, acquaintances and friends. Yet lunch and dinner, the maintenance of the house and the extensive family proceeded with ease and calm. The wife, throughout much of our culture, has been responsible for providing heirs and keeping the household orderly—as Beryl Graves did for years. She contains, it seems, the traditional woman of both patriarchial and matriarchial times, no less than necessary for the woman who would keep happy an ancient poet who lived in modern times.

A Conversation with Robert Graves

Juan Bonet/1969

From *La Estafeta Literaria*, 426-28 (September 15, 1969), 39-40. Translated by Richard D. Woods, Trinity University.

—What the public likes gives me an enormous pain.

—I prefer the most abused of my historical works.

I have moved. I think it's the French who say that moving is the same as a shipwreck at times followed by a fire. Yes, it is. The French are right.

And in this move for days I am surrounded by papers, papers, and papers. There have been moments of seriousness: helpless and discouraged about achieving order again, I was at the brink of throwing out everything. Meanwhile, there have been some exciting moments when I unexpectedly ran into something that I thought lost. Among my discoveries is a cache of interview notes with the poet Robert Graves, this adopted son of an island called Deyá. Graves like so many famous Englishmen turned out to be Irish.

From these old notes, some written by Graves himself, I reconstructed the interview, which has the value of something new and also a certain grace of perspective. When I did the interview some years ago, Graves had just come from Italy where he had been with Gide in Portofino, and I remember that he told me some cruel things about the French novelist.

During those years we usually found ourselves with Graves in a Palma cafe, "Figaro," now no longer standing. There the North American painter William S. Cook, one of the best friends of Gertrude Stein and the architect Le Corbusier, held forth. In Paris this architect built a house for Cook but it was destroyed in the so called "Big War."

"The whole house was glass," Cook would always say smiling and adding details.

At this cafe Graves would occasionally drop by. He was not then dressed in his very personal style as he goes now totally hippy and carrying a huge basket.

And then Graves had his own personal manner, very original, of being choleric but actually with great inner peace. (This is a bit confusing, but I don't know how to explain it better. What I mean is that Graves would grab you by the arm as though he meant to devour you. But then, full of tenderness, he would kiss you on the forehead and you would feel annointed and overcome.)

Graves wrote his best and his most mature work in Majorca. His novel, *I, Claudius*, translated into 16 languages, has sold more than several million copies. (I look at my notes and here is what he said to me about the novel): .

"No, it is not my favorite book. It is the favorite of the public, yes. I like the most abused ones of my historical works."

And then he explains it:

"I feel very sorry for the abused ones, yes. I will say, moreover, that I am a poet and I put very little value on my prose work."

(I look at my notes. It seems that I asked him about other poets, specifically about Eliot. Here are his reminiscences on that other famous poet):

"I met Eliot when we were boys. He was then a young barbarian, very revolutionary. I remember that he had green eyes . . . The last times that I was with him something happened that is worth telling. My manuscript on the "Muse" was ready and I offered it to a London publisher. He wasn't interested and a little later I found out that he committed suicide. The manuscript returned, I offered it to an American publisher. He also sent it back to me. A few months later he too took his own life. Then I offered my poor book to Eliot who was head of a famous English publishing house. He accepted it. A few months later, he received the Nobel Prize."

(From what I gather from my notes, taken during the conversation and amplified later by Graves's letter to Cook who was to pass it on to me, I tried to make the poet speak about the novel and some famous novelists themselves. Here are his responses to my questions):

"Do you think, Mr. Graves, that our period has representative novelists? Tell me which ones . . .

"The most disoriented. I will let you pick.

"Let us say that, in your opinion, there is no book, of the genre called the novel that represents the mood of our time . . ."

Graves's reply was delightful.

"Definitive? Do you mean less disoriented? It would be perhaps some dry treatise on geology, I don't know. Speaking of novelists, since that theme seems to interest you, I will say in talking about Englishmen and Americans, almost all of them want the big prize, a film success. They don't write novels, they write scenarios . . ."

(Concretely I spoke to him about Aldous Huxley, who precisely in that time was living in California and naturally was working on different scenarios for the screen. About Huxley the poet was cruel, even, in my opinion, a little bit unjust. This is what he said to me):

"Aldous Huxley is one of those writers who cannot forget the last thing that he has read. Ah! In the last years he feels a strange love for Greta Garbo and for the memory of Raquel Meller . . ."

(Afterwards I became interested in his work in progress because maybe he was doing a novel. He was working on a translation for UNESCO of a novel called "Enriquillo" by the Dominican author Manuel Galván. He praised the novel very much. Among my notes I find an opinion on Agatha Christie, the creator of detective novels. Graves referred to her telling me:

"We are talking about a very likeble woman. I was her neighbor. She was charming. Very superior to her work."

(Finally, making a frontal attack, I asked him about Spanish authors. His words are here):

"No, and no questions about Spanish politics either for I believe the two things are closely linked. I have lived in Spain since 1929 and I am always well treated. For this reason I don't want to criticize anyone or praise anyone. I am neutral."

(Nevertheless, he dared to mention the classics saying that he admired and knew some of them from the 15th and 16th centuries. About them he said):

"What I find to be too much is the rhetoric, the adornment. I work always trying to eliminate words from a paragraph. Everything that doesn't make the meaning clearer is unnecessary."

And here is this Robert Graves of a couple of years ago. His children, like his works, have been growing in Majorca, where also has grown the natives' admiration for him. Deyá, where he lives in the house of "Canellūn", has become the center of pilgrimages to the poet. There are more and more Americans who have selected Deyá, young poets or painters, in order to be near the master, several times nominated for the Nobel Prize. And a little while ago, filled with emotion, he thanked this Majorcan town for declaring him an adopted son.

One could say that in spite of all the problems, Graves, in getting a warm reception almost by popular acclamation from Deyá, was consoled in not receiving the Nobel Prize.

Flawed Science, Damaged Human Life:
An Interview with Robert Graves
Bruno Friedman/1969

From *Impact of Science on Society*, 20:4 (1969), 319-30. Reprinted by permission.

Interviewer: Mr. Graves, as a poet, classical scholar, and novelist whose books are based on the ancient Greek and Roman civilizations, you are particularly qualified to look at modern science from a historical perspective.

I'd like to start by referring to an intriguing remark you made in a letter addressed to *Impact* a few weeks ago. You wrote: 'Science ceased to be what it pretended to be, an idealistic search for wisdom, some time in the thirteenth century—though some insist on back-dating this to the twelfth.' What did you mean by that?

Graves: Just what I said. Science has lost its virgin purity, has become dogmatic instead of seeking for enlightenment and has gradually fallen into the hands of the traders. I was thinking of alchemy, which in its original form was a humble search for knowledge and truth based on intuition, but was gradually taken over by perverters and frauds who sought to persuade kings that they could turn base metal into gold.

Interviewer: And you feel that the motive of making money has dominated scientists, thus science, since that period?

Graves: It's only one of several irrelevant motives that have dominated science since that time.

There always have been scientists—seekers after wisdom—though for a long time they were not specifically identified as such. When they were first recognized as a separate class, in fact, they were called 'philosophers'—our current word 'scientist' being a rough translation of the word 'philosopher'.

Almost certainly, the earliest science was connected with the mystery religions, had become a part of the secret knowledge which the priests had to protect, conceal and never reveal.

Interviewer: As I remember it, in ancient civilizations—the Egyptian and Chaldean come immediately to mind—the storehouse of knowledge was the priesthood.

Graves: Just so. Science was once guarded by a secret society which nobody could join until he had satisfied certain tests that went beyond merely intelligence, tests of such qualities as sobriety, secrecy and the power to think in what may be called the fifth dimension, of which every true scientist should be capable even today.

Everywhere and on all occasions science seems to have begun as a secret storehouse of knowledge watched over by the few thinkers who felt complete trust and understanding of one another. Then gradually something went wrong. There was infiltration into this small society, some of its members yielding to the temptation of power or money or mundane interests other than the pure search for wisdom.

An early Greek philosopher—I can't remember his name, was it Anaxagoras?—was ridiculed by his friends for not meditating about practical things, but being particularly interested in meteorology— meaning the fanciful subject of weather, which everyone knew you can do nothing about. So one day, having foreseen good weather and therefore an immense harvest of olives, he quietly bought up all the local oil mills. Of course, when the harvest came along only he could press the oil, and he made a very large sum of money. In fact, this is the first record of money resulting from science, though then the scientist was not really interested in making money but only in defending himself against ridicule.

Interviewer: Then the baser motives entered science some time after the Hellenic period?

Graves: Long after. They did not appear in Islamic science and we eventually learned ours from the practical Perso-Arabic mystics named Sufis who had worked out their own scientific principles.

Interviewer: Certainly Islam was far ahead of Europe in science and learning in general until perhaps the fifteenth or sixteenth cen- tury and contributed much to European scholarship. Yet the roots of European science go back much farther, don't they? From Aristotle we got certain efforts at objective examination of facts and classifi- cation of existing knowledge. . . .

Graves: Aristotle was not an exact observer. He didn't realize that if you dropped a stone from the top of a tower it would move faster and faster as it went down.

Interviewer: Nobody did until Galileo around the beginning of the seventeenth century, 2,000 years later.

Graves: Yes, but Aristotle shouldn't have assumed that the stone went down at a constant rate.

Interviewer: Then you'd say that Aristotle was not a true scientist because he was not a good observer?

Graves: Yes. And there's another reason why I don't much care for Aristotle. He was a consummate logician. Well, my experience has set me against logic, because logic—from the Greek word, *logikon*—means 'something which has been arranged in words'. And rhetoric meant using the power of words—as his master Plato put it—to make the worse cause seem the better. Since words never wholly cover the phenomena to which they are applied those who rely on pure logic cannot be thinking truly.

Interviewer: Well, how do you think truly, Mr. Graves? What would you recommend as the alternative to logical thinking?

Graves: Thinking poetically.

Interviewer: Hmm . . . think poetically. At first glance, that, to a nonpoet, sounds like a strange and abstract idea. What exactly do you mean?

Graves: The top mathematicians and pure scientists whom I have known all think in the same way, which is in a sort of trance where logic doesn't rule.

Interviewer: Logic doesn't rule consciously, do you mean? The thinking is done at an intuitive level?

Graves: Yes. The process is explained in a recent book, which I've read in manuscript and I hope will be published quite soon, written by a French-Canadian named Lise La Frenière, who lives in Paris. Her view, with which I agree, is that all real thinking is done on a plane where there is no such thing as time. This view is a-logical, logic being purely three-dimensional; therefore a poet and a logician talk different languages.

Would you care to hear a poem I wrote the other day? We may call it a mathematical poem:

'Where is love when love is not?'
  Asked the logician.
'We term it *omega-minus*,'
  Said the mathematician.

'Does that mean marriage or plain hell?'
  Asked the logician.
'I was never at the altar',
  Said the mathematician.
'Is it love makes the world go round?'
  Asked the logician.
'Or, we might reverse the question,'
  Said the mathematician.

Now you know what omega-minus[1] is, don't you? It's where a thing is when it isn't. Poetry works on that same level.

Interviewer: Not much different from thinking scientifically, as you described it just previously—that is, thinking intuitively, with logic actually operating below the conscious level.

Graves: Reason rather than logic. Scientific thinking—the best scientific thinking—is thinking poetically.

Interviewer: That's poetic thinking for the scientists. How about poetic thinking as applied to the everyday lives of people?

Graves: Well, ordinary, simple, good people need to be protected against trouble and disaster. Originally their protection was the job of the poet, whether he was called a shaman, a philosopher, a mystic or whatever else. He watched against new intrusions that might come along to upset their lives. . . .

Interviewer: You mean the way that the outputs of modern science are rapidly changing people's lives?

Graves: Too rapidly. So, for example, when a steam-driven engine was invented for pumping water up to the top of the Pharos light-house, this was recognized as a dangerous precedent. If the slaves were denied their daily task of carrying water, they would grow lazy and they probably start rebellions. So the pump was neglected. It would have been pleasant watching the water being pumped up to the top of the tower, but after all it was much more proper for slaves to take it up in skins on their backs. The water-mill was similarly neglected.

I was thinking only this morning about a character mentioned by Suetonius who came before the Emperor Tiberius with a new type of glass goblet which he had invented. When the Emperor had handled and admired it the man purposely dropped it on the marble floor. It

neither cracked nor broke. Tiberius asked: 'Have you told your secret
to anyone?' 'No, Caesar, to nobody.' Tiberius turned to his guards:
'Cut off his head—glass like this will depreciate the price of gold.'

The lesson here is that certain inventions should be kept under the
control of the few sages who foresee the result of their exploitation.
Sages no longer exist as a class. The last time it would have been
possible to keep control of dangerous innovations was in the early
prime of the Royal Society. Its members were interested purely in
scientific knowledge and had a highly moral viewpoint—nor were
they even Catholics.

Interviewer: They were interested in science for its own sake, in
other words?

Graves: Yes, as a sort of moral force. The Royal Society is still one
of the few flickering beacons of scientific sanity, of interest in science
for its own sake.

Interviewer: How do you compare the other national scientific
societies or academies of science?

Graves: I can speak only from limited experience, but I would say
that most of them have been infiltrated by people who regard science
as either a nationalistic business or as a purely financial one. These
are men whom I would call the 'routineers' of science.

The main trouble, I feel, is that the men of broad vision, the true
creators and innovators, have long ceased to control the evolution or
uses made of science. I see no successors in sight, for example, for
such men as Cockcroft, Rutherford, Oliphant and Dalton.[2] Their
places get taken by bureaucrats with scientific training, not true
scientists. With their entry, science loses it moral motives and such
other motives as money, power and national or political objectives
replace them.

Interviewer: So, as you see it, one of the great problems of
modern science is that the outputs of science are diverted from moral
use. Any other flaws in the picture?

Graves: Another is the lessening of sound science—I might call it
'useful science'—and the growth of show-off science. Show-off
science encourages such evil things as shooting at the moon, an act
which outrages human sentiments all over the world.

Interviewer: A rather surprising experience we're having right
now at *Impact* seems to contradict this assertion, Mr. Graves. We

have received a number of manuscripts and interviewed a number of people for this particular number. Many of our contributors and interview subjects take up this very question of placing man on the moon. What is startling is that it is the people from developing countries, where there is the most poverty and great need for funds for development, who seem to be the most approving of the moon project, whereas the people from the more affluent countries, the technologically advanced countries, seem to be the more disapproving. You'd think it would be the reverse, wouldn't you?

Graves: Well, it reminds me of a man who leaves his wife and family to starve while he goes out and fights battles against strange foes. Until we have got this world in some sort of order, we should abstain from such expensive and dangerous nonsense. It is undertaken for purely nationalistic purposes, it doesn't serve human purposes as a whole. My dear friend Robert Frost, who was *the* American poet of his time, disapproved as strongly as I do about this shooting at the moon.

Interviewer: Mr. Graves, in our conversation before this interview began, you told me that you'd had a standard classical education at Oxford, with no scientific component. If you were starting your education all over again—or if you were advising a young writer still busy on his education—would this education include some grounding in science?

Graves: I hate conjectures. . . . Anyhow, I feel sorry for those at that age, especially my own children and grandchildren. Everything is in such a muddle for them. In the old days one could decide on a course for his life, for his future, or at least for his immediate future. But nowadays nobody knows what is going to happen: by the end of this very year we might all find ourselves in extremely doleful circumstances.

As to your question about getting some education in science, it depends on how science is taught, on whether it is taught the right way.

Interviewer: What do you mean by 'the right way'?

Graves: First of all, I mean that the teacher must insist that nothing must be taken for granted . . .

Interviewer: . . . which is one of the basic tenets of science . . .

Graves: . . . and next, he must remain human—if one doesn't remain human one can't think well.

Interviewer: We're back to this point of science and humanism again. How does a scientist or a teacher remain human?

Graves: By possessing a sense of humour, a real one, not a fake one. Unless one has a sense of humour he can't see the identity of opposites.

Interviewer: In two sentences you have made two provocative statements which I think we'd better follow up. First of all, what do you mean by a real sense of humour as opposed to a fake one?

Graves: Well, let me tell you two little jokes. The first of these has been making the rounds recently and is supposed to be very new, but actually dates back hundreds of years to the Nazr-al-Din stories of the Sufis.

A man comes into a bar and asks the bartender, 'Did you see me come in just now?' 'Yes, sir, I saw you come in'. 'Have you ever seen me before?' 'No, sir, I have not had that honour and privilege.' 'Then how did you know it was I?'

The second story is about the comedian, Foote. He was dining with a gentleman who showed him how to cut the skin of an orange so that it took the shape of a pig. Foote attempted to follow his instructions, but the results were most unfortunate. The gentleman raised an eyebrow at them and said, 'Sir, you have not made a pig, you have made a litter.'

The second story—though not too bad—is a mere play on words. It shows wit, but nothing else.

True humour is contained in the first story, which makes one think, if even for a fraction of a second. It raises a question, opens the eye, puts the commonplace in a novel setting because conventional equations of 'this equals that' are reversed. It presents new equations: 'this equals something else', with that 'something else' being often the very opposite of what is conventionally accepted.

Interviewer: Are we now on this matter of 'identity of opposites' which you mentioned a moment ago?—because I was just going to ask you about that.

Graves: That's exactly where we are. I remember talking once with Laura Riding, who was far the best poet of the Twenties. Laura said to me, 'You know, Robert, sometimes a poem reaches a point when you wonder just how can you set it exactly right. The answer very often is to add, in the right place, the simple word "not".' This was a very shrewd remark of Laura's.

I can make a mathematical analogy—and you must correct me here if I'm wrong because mathematics is not my own field. When you shift a quantity in a mathematical equation from one side of the equal sign to the other you change a plus sign to a minus sign, correct? Well, the minus sign is like 'not'—and the shift resulting in a 'not' gives you a new view of the matter.

Interviewer: This shifting operation, in fact, sometimes does give a new view when working with mathematical equations.

Graves: A 'not' can give you more than a strange and unusual point of view; it can make you think from the opposite point of view. In science, I'd say, if what you assert still holds true after you examined it from the new 'not' point of view, then you have a valid truth and not a false one.

The point is that the introduction of the 'not', the contradiction, the anomaly, not only reveals and tests truth, but is the very element of humour. *Quod erat demonstrandum.*

Interviewer: Let's talk more about science and human purposes. Do you feel, Mr. Graves, that a price is being paid for the material improvements that science and its offspring, technology, have brought to the human condition—I mean, a price in terms of effects, deleterious effects, on human values or on the quality of human life?

Graves: One bad effect lies in the very heart of science itself: I'm talking about scientists—or more particularly, scientists' wives. I've known a number of leading scientists and their wives, and regret having observed, as a generalization, that science takes a terrible toll of wives. There's more mental ill-health among the wives of scientists at the higher levels than anywhere else—which proves that something's wrong.

Interviewer: What form does this mental ill-health take?

Graves: A sense of frustration . . . because the husbands live in a world into which their women are not invited and which they feel is a dangerous world. The men live in an exclusive world in which things are viewed in a strange and different way. They cannot communicate with their wives about their work in the way open to most husbands.

The wives are excluded and, like all women isolated or barred from a large part of their husbands' lives, endure a cruel sort of loneliness.

Interviewer: This is because there is a high sense of dedication in these scientists?

Graves: Yes. But with dedication comes a kind of arrogance. This is not true of the finest scientists. I met Einstein once and had the feeling that he and his wife got on very well together. Einstein was different somehow. He was humble. The dedicated scientists who are also human are very few, but these are the best.

Mrs. Dalton[3]: Because they are human before they are scientists. An inhuman man cannot be a good scientist. All the really good scientists we've known get on very well with their wives—people like Cockcroft and Oliphant, whom my father mentioned just now. Because they are human they are good scientists and not merely cold scientists—professional, technological scientists.

Graves: What we mean seems to be that this latter bunch of professionals, who may be quite capable scientists, have been carried away out of orbit because they are insufficiently human. In a meta-phorical sense, you might say they are shooting at the moon and evading the human ties of earth.

Interviewer: Do you know of other human effects of science and technology—undesirable changes in ethical, cultural or social values or in behaviour?

Graves: Immense ones. Technology has destroyed the dignity of a man's labour—consider factories—and the warmth of the home. Modern technology condemns people to live in what aren't homes, but little life-boxes: three-roomed cubicles in great, blank city buildings. An unnatural environment. People can't live properly without trees. One of my favourite cities in the world is Sydney because there is a tree in practically every garden.

Interviewer: But is it technology or is it population increase that has resulted in people's being removed from a natural environment, from greenery and trees?

Graves: It is, I think, the technological treatment of population increase. The population is concentrated instead of being spread out, science and technology having provided the wrong social solution. And there would not have been this enormous flood of populations into cities but for the growth of technology, which started with the

Industrial Revolution around the middle of the eighteenth century.
Science and technology have themselves created the probem that
science and technology have been vainly trying to solve.

At the same time, the sense of honour and human dignity have
been sapped by the spread of technology. A man is no longer able to
be 'a man for a' that', as Robert Burns put it. He becomes a cog, a
number. You're aware of how constantly people are today treated as
numbers, in bank accounts, payroll records, electors lists, all aspects
of their human lives?

Interviewer: Very much aware. And of course, many people have
deplored the loss of individual dignity because of the loss of individual
craftsmanship with the advance of mass-production technology.

Graves: The trouble goes much deeper than that. The word
'genius' in one of its definitions means the 'distinctive character that
makes a thing what it is'. The 'genius of a man' originally meant his
manhood, that which makes him a man, and his sense of manhood
protects him against being demeaned, against the loss of his individ-
uality and personality. A man who had behaved wrongfully as a man
was said to have 'defrauded his genius'.

Well, the supply of real men is fast drying up because technology
takes care of all a man's desires and prevents him from making his
own decisions. His manhood, his genius, is diminished and lost.

My main objection to science, now that I think about it, is that it
has spoilt the relations between the sexes. All good life—and all
creativity—start with the gonads. Science and technology have
interfered with natural sexual expression by making men and women
no longer sure of themselves as men and as women, proud separate
complementary sexes. Women today are no longer sure of themselves as women but are forced to be auxiliary male personnel,
pseudo-males.

Waning of the male genius and the female wisdom . . . destruction
of male dignity and female dignity . . . the vanishing of the magic and
holiness of the female sex—and what follows? Total loss of sexual
assurance. Science and technology have diminished the romantic
relationship between the sexes and all but destroyed the pleasure and
joy of sex, which is where everything good in life starts.

I foresee a tremendous and imminent break-up of our technological world. But women recover more easily than men and will

doubtless take charge, as they have always done in times of catas-
trophe, and bring order out of the chaos.

[1]An extremely short-lived sub-atomic particle searched for and discovered in 1964 because
its existence had been predicted by a new physical theory.—Ed.

[2]The reference is to the brilliant physicists, Sir John Cockroft, Sir Ernest Rutherford, Dr.
Marcus Oliphant, and Dr. George C. J. Dalton.—Ed.

[3]Mrs. Catherine Dalton, Mr. Graves's daughter and the widow of the New Zealand atomic
physicist, Dr. George Clifford James Dalton, inventor of a nuclear fast-breeder reactor, was
present at the interview.

The Art of Poetry XI: Robert Graves
Peter Buckman and William Fifield/1969

From *The Paris Review*, 47 (1969), 119-45. Reprinted by permission.

Dressed in corduroys, mariner's sweater, black horsehide jacket, and with a blanket wrapped around his middle, Robert Graves rolled his own cigarettes and chain-smoked throughout the interview. Reading glasses hung from his neck on a ribbon which frequently became tangled in his hair. Tall, loosely built, Graves has always been physically powerful, but as result of a climbing accident during his schooldays he cannot swivel his head and therefore uses a reading stand—fidgeting it into strategic positions on the desk in front of him while he talked. Tins of small Dutch cigars, jars of tobacco, marbles, pencils and porcelain clown heads are on the desk. There is a carton brimming with press clippings on the floor. Over the fireplace is a shelf with the works of T.E. Lawrence; on the mantel, Greek, Roman, Oriental and African figurines. "This dial of wood? From a tree hewn in Shakespeare's yard." He fingered it, spoke of continuity. He knew Hardy, and Hardy knew

Gertrude Stein first told Robert Graves about Majorca. Except for the Civil War years, he has lived in Deyá since 1929. He and Laura Riding built the stone house he now occupies, and they lived in it together until 1936. There is an orchard with fifteen kinds of fruit trees, a large vegetable garden, and an English-style lawn of Bermuda grass.

Robert Graves is the author of over one hundred books, besides a number of anonymous rewrite jobs for friends. His most important prose work is *The White Goddess*, a history of poetic myth—"the language of poetic myth . . . was a magical language bound up with popular religious ceremonies in honour of the Moon Goddess, or Muse . . . and this remains the language of 'true' poetry . . . in the sense of being the unimprovable original, not a synthetic substitute." The true poet worships the White Goddess, or goddess of creation, unswerving and absolute devotion to

92

her is the poet's only path. He "falls in love, absolutely, and his true love for her is the Muse's embodiment." The present Muse is fifty-two years younger than Graves— "but we are the same age" . . . "I am at the top of my mania cycle because good things are happening to her just now." She is a classical dancer performing in a far-off city.

At various times during the following interview, he was setting the table, correcting a manuscript, checking references, cutting his nails with an enormous pair of scissors, picking carrots, singing folk songs, and slicing beans. He was not an easy man to keep up with.

Graves: Do you notice anything strange about this room?

Interviewer: No.

Graves: Well, everything is made by hand—with one exception: this nasty plastic triple file which was given me as a present. I've put it here out of politeness for two or three weeks, then it will disappear. Almost everything else is made by hand. Oh yes, the books have been printed, but many have been printed by hand—in fact some I printed myself. Apart from the electric light fixtures, everything else is handmade; nowadays very few people live in houses where anything at all is made by hand.

Interviewer: Does this bear directly on your creative work?

Graves: Yes: one secret of being able to think is to have as little as possible around you that is not made by hand.

Interviewer: You once wrote that "the Muse-poet must die for the Goddess as the Sacred King did when a divine victim." In spite of all you've survived, do you still hold to this?

Graves: Yes. What nearly always happens is that the Muse finds it impossible to sustain the love of a poet and allies herself with a pretended poet who she knows is not a real one. Someone she can mother. I have given a picture of it in a poem called "Lack." The process starts again each time that there's a death of love, which is as painful as a real death. There's always a murderer about, always a "Lack" character. The King or poet represents growth, and the rival or tanist represents drought.

Interviewer: Surely long years of service to the Muse are rewarded.

Graves: The reward is becoming eventually attached to somebody who's not a murderess. I don't want to talk about it, because I don't want to tempt my luck.

Interviewer: By definition your pursuit of the Muse cannot bring satisfaction. What has it given you?

Graves: It has brought me nearer and nearer to the center of the fire, so to speak.

Interviewer: Your poems, especially your love poems, get more intense as you go on. Is that a function of age, or experience?

Graves: One gets to the heart of the matter by a series of experiences in the same pattern, but in different colors.

Interviewer: In other words, you don't learn anything new, but you get a deeper understanding.

Graves: That's about it. An understanding of what the poet's ordeals are. Love poems must be bounced back off a moon. Moons vary. Love a different muse-woman and you get a different poem.

Interviewer: What about that simple appetite, lust, which you have attacked?

Graves: Lust involves a loss of virtue, in the sense of psychic power. Lust is giving away something that belongs to somebody else. I mean the act of love is a metaphor of spiritual togetherness, and if you perform the act of love with someone who means little to you, you're giving away something that belongs to the person you do love or might love. The act of love belongs to two people, in the way that secrets are shared. Hugs and kisses are permissible, but as soon as you start with what's called the mandalot—I invented the word, from the Greek; it comes from *mandalós* (which is the bolt you put in the socket) and means the tongue-kiss or by dictionary definition "a lecherous and erotic kiss"—you should reserve such familiarities only for those whom you really love. I'm on simple hugs-and-kisses terms with several friends. That's all right. But promiscuity seems forbidden to poets, though I do not grudge it to any non-poet.

Interviewer: Can the experience of the Muse give felicity?

Graves: Not really. But what does? Felicity and pain always alternate. She serves as a focus and challenge. She gives happiness. Here I use the English language precisely—hap: happening. She gives hap; provides happening. Tranquiliy is of no poetic use. (The first to use Muse in the sense of White Goddess was Ben Jonson—then it dropped down into weakly meaning self-inspiration of young men.)

After experience of the untranquil Muse one may move on to the Black Goddess—for black is positive in the East and stands for wisdom. Can a white Muse become a black one, or must it be another Muse? That is difficult . . .

Interviewer: They are all about of an age—

Graves: As a rule the Muse is one whose father has deserted her mother when she was young and for whom therefore the patriarchal charm is broken, and who hates patriarchy. She may grow to be very intelligent, but emotionally she is arrested at about the age of fourteen or fifteen.

Interviewer: What is the Muse's reaction to the poet?

Graves: It's embarrassing in a way for a well-known poet to write poems to a girl. She may resent being made a part of literary history. In France it is different. Many a woman wants to be known as the last girl Victor Hugo slept with . . . I'm all against literary history. Sometimes that's the reason why a "great poem," one that occurs in all the anthologies, is bad. It is usually interesting to examine its history.

Inteviewer: You mean it's been manufactured for an event?

Graves: Yes.

Interviewer: *The White Goddess* is a handbook and a shelter behind which all questions can be answered. Do you feel the need for a final definition of what you're up to?

Graves: *The White Goddess* and *The Nazarene Gospel Restored* are curious: I wrote the first to define the non-Jewish element in Christianity, especially the Celtic. And I wrote the second, with the help of the late Joshua Podro, to drive the Greek and Roman element out of what was a purely Jewish event. The curious result was that a special Early Christian Society got founded at Cambridge, based on the *Nazarene Gospel*, and various White Goddess religions started in New York State and California. I'm today's hero of the love-and-flowers cult out in the Screwy State, so they tell me: where hippies stop policemen in the street and say, "I adore you, officer." Also I get a number of letters from witches' covens, requesting flying ointment, magical recipes, and esoteric information.

Interviewer: In the *Colophon to Love Respelt* you talk of the battlefield being deserted. Who won?

Graves: I meant that there was no occasion for further poems on the subject. . . The historical sequence of a man's poems has a general resemblance to the order in which they are written. Yet often one writes a poem a long time before, or long after, a thing happens. Autobiography doesn't correspond exactly with poetic sequence.

Interviewer: You get the idea for a poem and then life catches up with it?

Graves: Or alternatively, you have omitted recording a poetic experience some time, and it occurs later. The words are already fixed in the storehouse of the memory. The poem is there at the origin, but at the seventh level of consciousness, and rises up gradually through each repeated revision. The rereading touches off the original hypnotic state, but expression is amplified.

Interviewer: In what way amplified?

Graves: For example, by the dreams of the night, which are the real interpretations in the primitive mind of the events of the previous day. A poem is nonetheless present from the conception, from the first germ of it crossing the mind—it must be scratched for and exhumed. There is an element of timelessness. The leading atomic scientist in Australia agreed with me the other day that time does not really exist. The finished poem is present before it is written and one corrects it. It is the final poem that dictates what is right, what is wrong.

Interviewer: Why did you not write war poems—of your trench experience in World War I like your friend Sassoon, and like Owen?

Graves: I did. But I destroyed them. They were journalistic. Sassoon and Wilfred Owen were homosexuals; though Sassoon tried to think he wasn't. To them, seeing *men* killed was as horrible as if you or I had to see fields of corpses of women.

Interviewer: Your poems are very complete and personal statements. Are you not at all reticent about what you reveal?

Graves: You tell things to your friends that you don't put into print.

Interviewer: But your audience . . .

Graves: Never use the word "audience." The very idea of a public, unless a poet is writing for money, seems wrong to me. Poets don't have an "audience": they're talking to a single person all the time. What's wrong with someone like Yevtushenko is that he's talking to thousands of people at once. All the so-called "great artists" were trying to talk to too many people. In a way, they were talking to nobody.

Interviewer: Hence your estimate of the English poets, whom you've criticized pretty heavily from the Poetry Chair at Oxford?

Graves: There are fifteen English poets—I am speaking precisely—in the history of listed literature who were real poets and not playing at it.

Interviewer: Would you care to name them?

Graves: That wouldn't be polite.

Interviewer: What do they have in common?

Graves: A source in the primitive. In the pre-rational.

Interviewer: As you work at a poem, do you feel that you are in some sense matching?

Graves: What happens is this—if a hypnotist says "look at this ring" and you are hypnotized by looking at the ring, then if he produces that ring again any time afterwards you go down. So also if you're writing a poem and you come back to it next day, you're immediately rehypnotized and at it again at that level.

Interviewer: Is it the physical circumstance? This room?

Graves: No, it's not the ambiance. The ambiance may help. It's the actual draft, which is yourself. That's the hypnotic ring.

Interviewer: And what happens if you don't "go down"?

Graves: That happened to me only yesterday. You can't force it intellectually. You spoil the poem. You mess it up. When you've worked through to the real poetic level, the connections webbing together every single word are quite beyond intellectual arrangement. A computer couldn't do it. You've got not merely sound and sense to deal with but the histories of the words, cross rhythms, the interrelation of all the meanings of the words—a complete microcosm. You never get it quite right but if you get it almost right it insulates itself in time. That's why real poems travel.

Interviewer: One feels your poetry has become more and more urgent, especially in the love lyrics which begin late.

Graves: Don't forget that I began in the Victorian Era; I had a lot to throw off. My poetic system accords with the Irish of the eighth century A.D., which was untinctured by Rome and which passed over eventually into Wales. Where did it come from? From the East. The correspondence with Sufic poetry is immense. That accounts for my interest in Omar Khayyám—a very noble poet so mishandled by FitzGerald. Besides, one gradually ceases to take critics into account.

Interviewer: Who got you to come to the Balearic Islands?

Graves: Gertrude Stein.

Interviewer: What did you think of her?

Graves: She had an *eye*. She used to say she had been the only woman in Picasso's life, that she had formed him. Maybe this was true; the other females were only round and about.

Interviewer: The poem you've shown me just now, *The Thing To Be Said*, seems to sum up so much.

Graves: Even in *The Thing To Be Said*, which I am working on now, which is about the necessity of first statement and that treats obsessive revision as a disease of age, there are ten successive versions. To date. Yes. The thing to be said, *say* it.

Interviewer: This immense, abrupt change. The late poetry—

Graves: Yes, that came when I was writing *The White Goddess*. (I wrote it in six weeks. It took me ten years to revise it. And I about tripled its length.) Suddenly I was answering ancient Welsh and Irish questions that had never been answered, and I didn't know how or why. It terrified me. I thought I was going mad. But those solutions haven't been disproved. Then someone sent me an article on the Irish tree alphabet and the footnote referred to Graves but not to me. It was my grandfather! And I hadn't even known he had investigated such things. I believe in the inheritance of skills and crafts—the inheritance of memory. They find now that if a snail eats another snail it gets that second snail's memory.

Interviewer: How did you sum up such vast detail into your conclusions?

Graves: I didn't. I knew it at the outset, and then checked.

Interviewer: You certainly write Muse poetry and express great contempt for the Apollonian, which I take it is the logical or utilitarian stuff, but aren't your novels Apollonian?

Graves: My writing of prose was always thematically in line with my thought. Always myself, I never left that. That was always the background. For example, *They Hanged My Saintly Billy* was to show how Victorian England really was: how rotten, how criminal in contrast to the received version. I had a couple of good characters too, besides the bad.

Interviewer: You write novels when stimulated by some historical problem. How do you go on from there?

Graves: I don't know. Some people have gifts, like a friend of mine who can balance a glass on his finger and make it turn round by just looking at it. I have the gift of being occasionally able to put myself back in the past and see what's happening. That's how historical novels should be written. I also have a very good memory for anything I want to remember, and none at all for what I don't want to remember. *Wife to Mr. Milton*—my best novel—started when my wife and I were making a bed in 1943 and I suddenly said: "You know, Milton must have been a trichomaniac"—meaning a hair-fetichist. The remark suddenly sprang out of my mouth. I realised how often his imagery had been trichomanic. So I read all I could find about him, and went into the history of his marriages. I'd always hated Milton, from earliest childhood; and I wanted to find out the reason. I found it. His jealousy. It's present in all his poems . . . Marie Powell had long hair with which he could not compete.

Interviewer: I think you describe that precisely in the novel, when they are riding on the heath . . .

Graves: He had the schoolmaster's disease. Constipation.

Interviewer: You mean that literally?

Graves: Yes! Of course I mean it literally! It shows in all his poetry. We know all about what he was given for it. Well, I had always smelt something, and then it all came to me more or less at once, and I wrote *Wife To Mr. Milton*. I found out a lot of things about him, heaven knows how, which have never been disproved.

Interviewer: Did he inherit the constipation?

Graves: He was a scrivener's son. He well may have.

Interviewer: How long did *I, Claudius* take to write?

Graves: *I, Claudius* and *Claudius the God* took me eight months. I had to get the job done quickly, because I was £4000 in debt. I got so close to him that I was accused of doing a lot of research that I had never done at all.

Interviewer: Did you dictate any of it?

Graves: No. I had a typist here in the village, but I didn't dictate. If you only use the main sources and you know the period, a book writes itself.

Interviewer: About how many hours per day did it take you?

Graves: I don't know. It must have been seven or eight. The story came to about 250,000 words in all. I had mortgaged the house and didn't want to lose it.

Interviewer: Why did you choose the historical novel?

Graves: Well, with that one I had noted in my diary, a year or two before, that the Roman historians—Tacitus, Suetonius and Dion Cassius but especially Tacitus—had obviously got Claudius wrong, and that one day I'd have to write a book about it. If I hadn't done so you wouldn't be here drinking in this house.

Interviewer: What did you have in mind at the end of *Claudius the God*? There's a distinct change in Claudius. One wonders what you were getting at as a novelist?

Graves: I didn't think I was writing a novel. I was trying to find out the truth of Claudius. And there was some strange confluent feeling between Claudius and myself. I found out that I was able to know a lot of things that happened without having any basis except that I knew they were true. It's a question of reconstructing a personality.

Interviewer: There is not much direct source extant, though he wrote voluminously.

Graves: There's his speech to the Aeduans, his letter to the Alexandrians, and a number of records of what he said in Suetonius and elsewhere. We know now exactly what disease he suffered from: Little's disease. The whole scene is so solid, really, that you feel you knew him personally, if you're sympathetic with him. The poor man—only now, at last, people have begun to forget the bad press he was given by contemporary historians. And he's now regarded as one of the very few good emperors between Julius Caesar and Vespasian.

Interviewer: In the end, though, he was disenchanted—

Graves: He saw he could do nothing. He had to give up.

Interviewer: He disintegrated and became very nearly another Caligula or Tiberius . . .

Graves: Well, now—Caligula was born bad. Tiberius was a marvelous man. But too much pressure was put on him and he warned the Senate of what was going to happen. He foresaw a severe psychological breakdown. If you've always been extremely clean—always brushed your teeth, and made your bed—and you get to a point of intolerable stress, you break down and display what is called paradoxical behavior: you mess your bed, you do the most disgusting things. Tiberius had been noted for his chastity and manly virtues, and then he broke down. I now feel the greatest possible sympathy for Tiberius.

Interviewer: Weren't you getting at Livy a bit in the novel as a manipulator of truth for effect?

Graves: It's sort of habit in my family, you know. My granduncle was Leopold von Ranke, the so-called "father of modern history." He was always held up to me by my mother as the first modern historian who decided to tell the truth in history.

Interviewer: Did that instigate your quest, the shibboleths you've upset to the consternation of many?

Graves: You see there are many people who believe things of which they can't get rid. Suddenly they are faced by some strange fact—such as that God, in the Holy of Holies, had a wife. My friend Raphael Patai has worked it all out in his *Hebrew Goddess*. It's more than they can stand. But you've got to admit it.

Interviewer: That God had a wife? Did you really mean that?

Graves: Indeed he did. It's in the Talmud. Of course the Jews had always kept it rather quiet. At first he was One—but then came the division. You've got to find the focal point. God was a male deity and the focal point was obviously a woman. He couldn't do without one.

Interviewer: How many books have you published?

Graves: One hundred and twenty-one—but many of those are revised collections. Then I've written books for other people.

Interviewer: Why have you done that?

Graves: Because they had something to say and they couldn't write it down.

Interviewer: Have you given up writing fiction?

Graves: It might happen again. I doubt it, but I don't know. One never knows.

Interviewer: After writing *The Reader Over Your Shoulder* with Alan Hodge in 1942—your handbook for writers of English prose—you say that your own style changed completely. Why, or rather how?

Graves: Whoever thinks about the English language and tries to discover its principles, and also pulls a whole lot of writers to pieces to show how badly they write, can't afford to write badly himself. In 1959, I entirely rewrote *Goodbye To All That*—every single sentence—but no one noticed. Some said: "What a good book this is, after all. How well it's lasted." It hasn't lasted at all. It's an entirely new product. One of those computer analyses of style couldn't possibly decide that my historical novels were all written by the same hand. They're completely different in vocabulary, syntax and language-level.

Interviewer: Considering this vast output and all the revision, how much time do you spend writing? Do you write everything by hand?

Graves: Yes. Now let me see, *Nazarene Gospel Restored* took me two years. Now that is 800 pages of close writing. Yes, it's about— two books a year for 50 years. That's not so much. I have nothing else to do. The score this year is six.

Interviewer: Do you find you can remember that vast research you have collected?

Graves: I know where to look.

Interviewer: Isn't it difficult to be here so far from libraries?

Graves: I have never worked in a library.

Interviewer: Where do you get all this information?

Graves: I don't know. It comes. I am not erudite. In the normal way of being I am not even well-read. I am simply well informed in certain areas of my interest.

Interviewer: You have to know the dates of history—the spelling of the Welsh words—

Graves: I've got a Welsh dictionary. I've got quite a big classical library.

Interviewer: Would you say the core ideas come first and then you research?

Graves: One has the whole vision of the thing—and then one just checks. Cause may not necessarily ordain effect; it may equally be that effect ordains cause—once one has got the whole time thing under control.

Interviewer: What do you do exactly?

Graves: Revise the manuscript till I can't read it any longer, then get somebody to type it. Then I revise the typing. Then it's retyped again. Then there's a third typing, which is the final one. Nothing should then remain that offends the eye.

Interviewer: This is for prose?

Graves: Yes. But that's no proof that in ten years' time it may not read badly. One doesn't know about prose at the time.

Interviewer: And poetry?

Graves: Sometimes you know: "This is right, this is one of the things that stands." You feel there are a certain number of poems that have got to be written. You don't know what they are, but you feel: this is one, and that is one. It is the relation between jewels and the matrix—the jewels come from the matrix, then there's the matrix to prove it. A lot of poems are matrix rather than jewels.

Interviewer: What do you mean?

Graves: The matrix is partly jewel, partly not jewel. And lots of poems are like that. Those are the ones that usually the public likes best: ones that are not wholly jewels.

Interviewer: Is that because these poems are transitional between generalized views and your personal attitude?

Graves: Something like that.

Interviewer: More accessible?

Graves: Yes.

Interviewer: Do you still experiment with hallucinogens?

Graves: I had two trips on the Mexican mushroom back in 1954 or so. None since. And never on LSD. First of all it's dangerous, and secondly ergot, from which LSD is made, is the enemy of mankind. Ergot is a minute black fungus that grows on rye, or did in the Middle Ages, and people who ate rye bread got manic visions, especially Germans. They now say that ergot affects the genes and might disorder the next generation. It occurs to me that this may explain the phenomenon of Nazism, a form of mass hysteria. Germans were rye-eaters, as opposed to wheat-eaters like the English. LSD reminds me of the minks that escape from mink-farms and breed in the forest and become dangerous and destructive. It has escaped from the drug factory and gets made in college laboratories.

Interviewer: You have spoken of a vision of total knowledge that you once had at twelve—

Graves: You probably had a similar vision, and you've forgotten it. It needn't be a vision of anything; so long as it's a foretaste of Paradise. Blake had one. All poets and painters who have that extra "thing" in their work seem to have had this vision and never let it be destroyed by education. Which is all that matters.

Interviewer: You've just finished a new translation of the *Rubáiyát* of Omar Khayyám. Why did you choose the *Rubáiyát*, rather than the work of a purer Sufic poet such as Rumi or Sa'adi?

Graves: I was invited to cooperate in the task by Omar Ali-Shah, whose family has possessed the original manuscript since A.D. 1153. That's why. I was in the hospital and very glad of the job to take my mind off hospital routine. Khayyám's original poem was written in honor of God's love, and spiced with satires against the Moslem puritans of the day. FitzGerald got it all wrong: he believed Khayyám really was a drunkard, and an unbeliever, not a man who was satirizing unbelievers. It's amazing how many millions have been fooled by FitzGerald. Most of them will hate being undeceived.

Interviewer: You have said that the critics now writing about your *Rubáiyát* fail to understand it because they are not Sufis.

Graves: As I said, I can take no credit for the job. I worked from a literal crib by Omar Ali-Shah, who is a Sufi. Not only a Sufi, but his family is in the direct line of descent from the Prophet—and they claim that Mohammed was a Sufi and delivered this secret doctrine to them.

Interviewer: It seems to me your Khayyám is more clear and incisive intellectually, whereas FitzGerald—

Graves: FitzGerald, you see, was one of those Irishmen at a time when people were ashamed of being Irish and so kept it quiet. And he became a sort of dilettante Englishman. And broke with the poetic tradition of Ireland, which is one of the strongest in the world. I should think after the Persian it is the strongest.

Interviewer: You are talking about the original Irish poetic tradition?

Graves: There is only one!

Interviewer: You explained to me once that that was originally Sufi—

Graves: Before that it was Milesian Greek superimposed on the archaic Libyan culture of about 2500 B.C. The Milesians came to Ireland via Spain and brought with them the Ogham tradition— which is an early form of alphabet, taking us back toward the day when letters originated in the observation of flights of cranes, and so on. But Ireland always remained in contact with Greek-speaking Antioch and not Rome, which was important.

Interviewer: Is the important thing that Ogham was pre-classical?

Graves: That's right. Before Plato. Before the Greeks went wrong. You know, the Jews had a saying—"of the ten measures of folly the Greeks have nine." They were all right until about the sixth century

B.C. By the time of Alexander the Great they'd gone to pieces altogether.

Interviewer: In what way?

Graves: They tried to decry myth. They tried to put in its place what we would now call scientific concepts. They tried to give it a literal explanation. Socrates jokes about myths and Horace makes fun of them. When put to it, Socrates could clarify a myth in a way that deprived it of all sense. They simply had no use for poetic thought. Logic works at a very high level in consciousness. The academic never goes to sleep logically, he always stays awake. By doing so, he deprives himself of sleep. And he misses the whole thing, you see. Sleep has seven levels, topmost of which is the poetic trance—in it you still have access to conscious thought while keeping in touch with dream . . . with the topmost fragments of dream . . . you own memory . . . pictorial imagery as children know it and as it was known to primitive man. No poem is worth anything unless it starts from a poetic trance, out of which you can be wakened by interruption as from a dream. In fact, it is the same thing.

Interviewer: But where does this itself come from?

Graves: From yourself, under the direction of the more-than-you formed by your relation with the person with whom you are in rapport at the time. If anybody were really observant he'd be able to take a poem and draw a picture of the person it was addressed to.

Interviewer: In looking at the beloved do you then see yourself most clearly—as distinct from looking at yourself?

Graves: Yes. Otherwise it's not you.

Interviewer: How do you feel about honors and laureateships? Will you accept if the laureateship is offered to you?

Graves: I don't answer questions about conjectures. I don't want any honors but I wouldn't so much mind being honored for writing novels which sell abroad and earn money for England. Writing poems is different. To get a C.B.E. for being a poet would be absurd. But the Government always tries to coax well-known writers into the Establishment; it makes them feel educated . . . I refuse doctorates, because they suggest that one has passed some sort of academic test. Accepting the Professorship of Poetry at Oxford was different—it's a free election.

Interviewer: In your last and most violent lecture at Oxford you said there were no poetic standards left. It is rare for you to make generalizations of this sort. Do you feel that "pop" poetry is inconsistent with dedication to the Muse?

Graves: There are no standards of verse-craft left, I think I said. Genuine folk-songs are welcome, but why those artificial songs of protest? There are few now, if any, who go to the real root of the thing. Fewer, since Frost and Cummings died.

Interviewer: What about your own poetic influences, apart from the Tudor poet Skelton and Laura Riding?

Graves: "Influence" is a very loose term. It sounds as though one is being dominated by someone. I never wrote anything in Laura Riding's style as far as I know. I learnt from her a general attitude to things, rather than verse-craft.

Interviewer: Is it that what you get from successive incarnations of the Muse?

Graves: Yes, but in the form of warnings rather than instructions.

Interviewer: May I ask you about the way you work? You don't have a routine, do you?

Graves: None. I admit only to a certain sense of priority in things. This morning for instance I got up at seven. I felt drawn to the ash pit where I burn waste paper and sieved out all tins and things which have been mistakenly put there. Then I put the ash on the compost heap. Then I soaked the carrot patch so that I could thin it out a bit. Then I revised my "Monsters" piece.

Interviewer: You write in longhand, on a sort of lectern . . .

Graves: That's because I broke my neck once. When the doctor asked me how, I couldn't remember until just the other day. It was when I was climbing Snowdon in 1913. I was belayed in a gully when the leader dislodged a large stone: it fell on my head and knocked me out. The other day I had almost exactly the same experience and so remembered the occasion. Now my neck is—well, I wrote a poem about it: "Broken Neck."

Interviewer: Does most of your income come from royalties on your novels?

Graves: I don't know, really. I never study my royalty returns.

Interviewer: You said you only read for information. What do you read and when do you get time?

Graves: I used to read at night, now I go straight to sleep. I don't read for pleasure. The other day I had to revise *The Nazarene Gospel Restored* for publication in Hungary, which meant a good deal of research.

Interviewer: You said, "I foresee no change for the better in the world until everything gets worse." Well, now it *is* worse. Can we do anything about it?

Graves: Poets can't march in protest or do that sort of thing. I feel that it's against the rules, and pointless. If mankind wants a great big final bang, that's what it'll get. One should never protest against anything unless it's going to have an effect. None of those marches do. One should either be silent or go straight to the top. Once this village was without electricity for three months because the local system had broken down and the provincial company was scared of putting a pylon on the land of an old noblewoman, whose son was a Captain-General and who said that the spot was sacred to St. Catalina Tomás, the island's patron saint. I went to Madrid to see the Minister of Information and National Tourism, and told him, "The local hotels will be empty this summer for lack of electricity." He kindly informed our Civil Governor that the pylon should be put up regardless of the Saint's feelings. But it's different if one can't go to the top. I regret the war in Vietnam, but marching won't stop it, and there is no one person, like our Minister in Madrid, who can control this complex situation.

Interviewer: Does this disturb you?

Graves: Civilization has got further and further from the so-called "natural" man, who uses all his faculties: perception, invention, improvisation. It's bound to end in the breakdown of society, and the cutting down of the human race to manageable size. That's the way things work; they always have. My hope is that a few cultural reservations will be left undisturbed. A suitable place might be certain Pacific Islands, and tracts in Siberia and Australia, so that when the present mess is over, the race of man can restore itself from these centers.

Interviewer: Who will be on the reservations? Who'll decide?

Graves: The people who are already there. They should be left. The Melanesians, for instance and the palaeo-Siberians.

Interviewer: Has your living here in Deyá isolated from what you call the modern mechanarchic civilization gradually led to what you call handcraft in your poetry?

Graves: I once lived here for six years without moving out. That was in the years 1930-1936. Didn't even go to Barcelona. Apart from that, I've always made a point of traveling. One's got to go out, because one can't live wholly in oneself or wholly in the traditional past. One's got to be aware of how really nasty urban life is.

Interviewer: But you take in much less by osmosis than if you were T. S. Eliot at the bank?

Graves: Obviously I do.

Interviewer: You are constantly revising your collected poems. Why?

Graves: I realize from time to time that certain poems were written for the wrong reasons, and feel obliged to remove them; they give me a sick feeling. Only the few necessary poems should be kept. There's no mystery about them: if one is a poet, one eventually learns which they are. Though of course a perfect poem is impossible. Once it had been written, the world would end.

Speaking Freely
Edwin Newman/1970

From *Difficult Questions, Easy Answers* (Garden City: Doubleday, 1973), 190-213. Reprinted by permission.

Mr. Newman: Hello, I'm Edwin Newman. Today Robert Graves is 'Speaking Freely'. Mr. Graves, poetry, for you, seems not to be simply a technical mastery of words; but a way of living and thinking. Can you define it?

Mr. Graves: It's somewhat monastic in a way, bound by all sorts of private rules. So you want to pry into my secrets?

Mr. Newman: Yes, very much so, yes.

Mr. Graves: Well, let's begin from when I left the Army early in 1919, having already published three books of poems, and decided never to be anybody's stooge for the rest of my life. That was rather a boastful decision; but I've never accepted a job since—apart from two professorships. One, five years later, was the professorship of English at Cairo University, Egypt. There I was responsible only to the Vice-Chancellor and I had no predecessors or assistants—in fact I had to buy all the books for the Library. . . . The next job was forty-five years later, when I went to Oxford as Poetry Professor, for private reasons entirely unconnected with the job. There again, I was responsible to nobody except the Vice-Chancellor; and both he and his successor had been undergraduates at the same time as myself, so I had nothing to fear. Apart from that, I have never been anybody's stooge—a very comfortable feeling. What is more, I have never written for any market but my own.

Mr. Newman: So you've never written for any market but your own? You really write for yourself? Do you have anybody in mind, then, when you sit down to write? You have written, I find, 125 books, including poetry. Some of them were surely written with a particular market in mind, even if the poetry was not?

Mr. Graves: A poem is always written for some particular person.

And I was asked this same question by Malcolm Muggeridge in a B.B.C. interview.

Mr. Newman: I know him.

Mr. Graves: Good! He asked me: 'Mr. Graves, are the women to whom you write your poems real or imaginary?' And I answered: 'Well, Malcolm, if you want any telephone numbers, you're not going to get them.' That ended that.

Mr. Newman: But to elaborate on this point, Mr. Graves, you must have written about what rewards a poet must expect? You set out at the end of the first World War never to take orders from anybody? But you do, in effect, take orders from your personal Muse, surely? The character whom you call the White Goddess?

Mr. Graves: That's rather a difficult question. I spent ten years writing a book called *The White Goddess*, and the other day, reading the *Sunday Times*, I found myself listed amongst the thousand 'Makers of the Twentieth Century'—in the G-H section, along with Goebbels, Goering and Hitler. I wondered what I'd done, and found that I had written *The White Goddess*. It was not my only book, but had just got around a bit more than the rest. And 'The White Goddess' is a historic character: the goddess of love and battle, the goddess of life and death, who ruled Europe long before any male gods appeared here. She was a hard taskmistress and kept her male subjects in very good order; until eventually they broke allegiance after the arrival of our Indo-European ancestors from Central Asia, who were cattle people. Cattle people have gods, not goddesses, for the simple reason that the bull rules a herd, and that the cows count on him for protection. Any challenger for the headship has to meet the horns of the king bull; so also with cattle kings and their challengers. Those cattle people did no planting, but simply drifted from one pasture to the other. The whole fertility mystique in Europe and other parts of the world where nomadic patriarchal herdsmen are not found, is dependent on agriculture. The woman's job is to plant, sow and harvest. She alone has the right touch, is at one with nature and knows exactly what to do. So, when these two opposed cultures mix, there's great confusion at first.

The White Goddess had to keep firm control of men; otherwise they would soon have got out of hand. And she did so for a long time. Few people realize that this same Goddess, under the name of Ashera, was in charge of Jerusalem until long after the earlier books of the Bible had been written; and that she had a temple on the Temple hill about five times the size of Jehovah's. And that she took all political decisions herself until she found at last that she could no longer trust men, and decided: 'Very well, let them see how they can manage by themselves.' And so she retreated. She is still always there privately for those who need her, in the person of the Virgin Mary or of the woman whom one adores; but politically she has stepped aside and let men make a mess of things.

I was asked to give the annual address at the London School of Economics recently, and was rather puzzled why. They asked me to name my subject. So I told them: 'Mammon'. They wrote back complaining that they did not know what Mammon was. I thought it a little odd: must I explain simply that Mammon was the Hebrew word for money and that the Talmud was quite clear on the subject? There are two sorts of Mammon: the Mammon of righteousness and the Mammon of unrighteousness. In the Gospels, only the Mammon of unrighteousness is mentioned. And the Mammon of righteousness was exemplified when Abraham bought the cave of Machpelah from Ephron the Hittite to be a burial place for all Israelite patriarchs descended from him—that was a righteous use of money. Then came the unrighteous use of money, when Joseph's brothers sold him to the Midianites in the desert. Money, in fact, was neither good nor bad in itself at the start but must be put to good use. What eventually happened was that money ceased to be either good or bad, and became just bad—a self-sufficient and conscienceless god.

Mr. Newman: Do you think this is because we have gods rather than goddesses?

Mr. Graves: Women always say: 'I'm such a fool about money.' Meaning: 'I don't want to hear anything about it because it's a bad thing, however convenient at times. As soon as you work for money and nothing but money, you might as well be dead.'

Mr. Newman: Well let me, if I may . . .

Mr. Graves: That's a poetic view, and unarguable.

Mr. Newman: Well, all right; let me push on with it! You've taught—you said you've only twice been a professor, but you have nevertheless lectured at a number of American universities.

Mr. Graves: I get around, yes, because I'm interested in what's happening in America.

Mr. Newman: After one visit you spoke of 'those talented, beautiful, well-groomed, studious girls and their dreadful, ignorant loutish escorts with nothing to talk about except the ballgame.'

Mr. Graves: That was at. . .

Mr. Newman: Now, if in this unfortunate money-directed society the men are mostly louts, how do the women escape being so?

Mr. Graves: Escape being *louts*? 'Lout' is a male term. That was some years ago. I don't know what's been happening since. And to judge from some of the characters who come here, what you call 'loutishness' seems to have caught on pretty well.

Mr. Newman: What I'm asking is: in the society which we now live in, which is god-rather than goddess-dominated, do women come out of it better than men do?

Mr. Graves: (*pause*) I'd like to have notice for that question. It's too big a one.

Mr. Newman: You once said: 'If I were a girl, I'd despair. The supply of good women far exceeds that of the men who might deserve them.' Do you . . .

Mr. Graves: Oh, yes I do. . . . The fact is that for one reason or another homosexuality among men has gone so far that it's very difficult now for a woman to find a man who isn't in some way tainted with it. I suppose that it's partly due to heredity, partly to environment, but largely because men now drink too much milk.

Mr. Newman: Really?

Mr. Graves: It's a fairly widespread medical view.

Mr. Newman: Well, that would make homosexuality rampant in the United States . . .

Mr. Graves: That percentage is, I read, about twenty times what it should be. Normally, it's about 1.5 per cent of the population. Homosexuality was recognized by the American Indians: they had *bardashes* who had been allowed to decide at the age of thirteen or fourteen that they wanted to become women. So they were allowed to dress and behave as such. Fair enough! What happens now is that men pretend to be men but are not. And wives soon find that their husbands are really more interested in the other thing . . . which is enough to break up almost any home.

Mr. Newman: Mr. Graves, is your supposition, or belief, that plentiful milk drinking causes homosexuality, based on intuition or on what we call scientific observation?

Mr. Graves: On objective reasoning. Unfortunately a lot of men gain the confidence of unsuspecting girls by being partly women themselves. They learn all the dirty tricks that used to be played by women on nasty men, and use them against women.

Mr. Newman: Do you despair of American society? For example, you wrote quite recently about—this is a quote—'the marked decline in native American genius since the turn of the century', you were then blaming it on the educational system which, you said, was too logical. In your view—and you go to the United States quite often— are we in serious danger? I ask this question very seriously.

Mr. Graves: I think the young people are all right, in so far as they haven't drunk too much milk or allowed themselves to be drugged into imbecility—as too many of the weaklings have—but there's a good base of sense among the best of the young. Oddly enough, they know far more about mathematics than my generation, and also more than the intermediate generation. I like them, I must say.

Mr. Newman: Of course, the United States is a country where what we call urbanization has gone very far—though possibly in England it's gone just as far. You think urbanization is a very, very unfortunate thing, do you not? You don't like living in a city yourself and you think city life has a very bad effect on most people and in particular on poets? Is that right?

Mr. Graves: The two things don't go too well together.

Mr. Newman: Then let's talk about urbanization, and about the values that city life creates. You say, for example, that most modern American poems are dull because most American poets live in cities.

Mr. Graves: I have said nothing of the sort. I say that the whole craftsmanship of poetry has gone down the drain, throughout the country, in the same way as craftsmanship in painting has gone down the drain. In painting academies you're allowed to paint how and what you like, and claim that it's glorious and wonderful. And if you can persuade a gallery to buy your pictures or sculptures, very well, that proves it. As for poems, the actual quality of writing has enormously declined since the time of, say, Robert Frost and E. E. Cummings, who were both very, very careful writers. There are one or two real poets still around—I won't name them, so as neither to encourage nor discourage them—who are working honestly and well. But as Robert Frost once said: 'It's fun playing tennis without a net, but it's not so good a game.'

Mr. Newman: And that is what . . .

Mr. Graves: If you're writing a poem and you want to have any effect on your readers . . . though you should not really be thinking of your readers, but only of yourself as your own reader—you've got to put them under the hypnotic trance in which you yourself write poems. And you impose this trance by certain hidden technical aids in the use of words and language; but to find this out takes years and years. If I write a poem and feel dissatisfied with it—which I almost always am—I re-write it anything from five to thirty-five times. Twelve is a good average. I finish the draft at night; in the morning I wake up and it looks quite different. So I have been doing the repair work in my sleep, and I now know more or less what's wrong. This may happen three or four nights running, the poem getting each time more and more like what it was originally going to be.

Mr. Newman: This is something which you impose on yourself: the trance in which poetry is written?

Mr. Graves: One doesn't impose it; one suddenly finds it . . . have you ever suffered from migraine? Well, I suffer from frequent migraines. In fact, I've written a poem saying that love is a universal migraine. Now, where was I? I've interrupted myself.

Mr. Newman: You were talking about the trance in which poems are written and the technical methods by which the trance may be induced or imposed.

Mr. Graves: The poem attacks you in the same way as a migraine does. You are looking at a page and all at once you can't read clearly and you realize you've got a migraine. Gradually the whole bright semi-circle of light expands, and you can see nothing. Which is how a poem starts. It forces itself upon you, and then you must go on fighting until it's gone.

Mr. Newman: Do you sit down every day in the hope that inspiration will come, or with the intention of inducing it?

Mr. Graves: No, a poem is completely unforeseeable. Very often one is deceived and makes a mess of things; it doesn't very often happen, but usually the poem comes out all right, if you persevere. But it must have that clear internal order in which every single word corresponds with every single other—and, remember, words must not be treated as counters, which usually happens, but as living things. Now, here I have this thirteen-volume *Oxford English Dictionary*, and also that *Slang Dictionary* and that *English Dialect*

Dictionary in six volumes and *Noah Webster* and Latin, Greek, Welsh, Irish, French, Spanish, Majorcan and German dictionaries. I'm always thinking about the history of words. Every word carries a long history of usage with it, and combines creatively with thousands of others all along its line. A poem is a most fantastic experience.

Mr. Newman: Mr. Graves, if that is the case, does one improve as a poet as one grows older? Since there is always more to call on?

Mr. Graves: Most poets have finished by the age of twenty-three. It's very rare indeed for anyone to go on until the age of forty-six, as Shakespeare did. It's still rarer to find a case like Hardy, who stopped writing poems for several decades then picked it up again in his sixties and went on to the eighties. As a rule, poetry is part of one's adolescent love affairs only.

Mr. Newman: Are you saying there, sir, that people stop writing, or that they simply don't write as well after youth has gone?

Mr. Graves: They don't write poems.

Mr. Newman: They don't write poems at all?

Mr. Graves: No, they don't write poems, though they often write verse. They cease to be poetically alive.

Mr. Newman: In your own case . . .

Mr. Graves: Forty-six is the dangerous year.

Mr. Newman: Forty-six?

Mr. Graves: Forty-six is the year in which most people have nervous breakdowns; be very careful. . . . I won't ask your age!

Mr. Newman: I don't have to worry about that any more but . . .

Mr. Graves: Anyhow, forty-six—that was once the age in which everybody was due to die and still is in the jungles of Africa. And it was so in England in Elizabethan days. And Nicholas Lord Vaux, quoted by Shakespeare, wrote: 'I loathe that I did love in youth that I thought sweet' at the age of forty-six. He said: 'For age with stealing steps hath clawed me with her crutch, And lusty life away she leaps as there had not been such . . . The noble shroud . . . the winding sheet. . . .' He was ready for the grave. And so was Shakespeare when he retired at that same age. Now, forty-six (be very careful) is the age when businessmen have nervous breakdowns. They go off to a hospital and at the end of a year or two they feel recovered. They want to come back but as a rule they've lost their jobs. It's very cruel.

Mr. Newman: In your own case, Mr. Graves—which I think it is

impossible to avoid asking about—forty-six was nearly thirty years
ago for you, and you are certainly still writing poetry. And twenty-
three was more than half a century ago.

Mr. Graves: I was never afraid of death—having already officially
died of wounds in France on my twenty-first birthday—and I was
never afraid of losing my job—I hadn't a job to lose.

Mr. Newman: Does moneyed success spoil a poet?

Mr. Graves: People say there's no money in poetry: but on the
other hand there's no poetry in money. And I used to be careful once
never to make more money on my poems than would keep me in
cigarettes. And then—well, my numerous children and grandchildren
had to go to college, and I eventually found out, to my surprise, that
the detritus, the residue, the cast-off stuff, namely the work-drafts,
were worth far more than the published poems. So I was able to
send those children to college and live quite well myself by selling
what I might easily have thrown away but had kept. Why I kept my
drafts is easily explained: it was because when one gets to the end of
a poem, one looks back to make sure that nothing important has
dropped out on the way. I put the drafts aside, and let them pile up;
and finally sent them up to the attic.

Mr. Newman: Has it helped you, Mr. Graves, that you've had two
families? I know you have said that it is a very good thing for there to
be considerable distance in years between parent and child.

Mr. Graves: Well, you've just seen my son, Tomás—he's sixteen
and I'm now in my seventy-fifth year. I became a great-grandfather
two years ago—but I don't take it too seriously. Old age is a pure
illusion. (*pause*) Centuries are like men. We start off with tremendous
ringing of church bells when the New Century comes in—everything's going to be wonderful! And then we have sympathetic
growing pains and by the Forties or Fifties we settle down into the
century. After that, things turn nasty. And by the time the century
reaches threescore and ten we can expect 'labour and heaviness' as
the Psalmist said. And everyone starts worrying what's going to
happen in the year 2000 with the population explosion and a general
break-down. All that one can say is that nowadays there are glasses
manufactured to improve your sight, which was denied King David
when he wrote about the labour and heaviness due at the age of
seventy. And now you also can get dentures. The Father of the

United States, General Washington, invented and made them himself
. . .

Mr. Newman: Of wood, I believe.

Mr. Graves: Yes, and the only trouble was that he couldn't control
the spring, so that his mouth was always in danger of flying open.
That's why he got the reputation for such noble taciturnity. But
anyhow, what the century wants now is sight: in order to investigate
its personal problems and find out exactly who is befouling the state.
We all know quite well who he is really, but we don't say so. We also
need teeth to implement our laws; we're now in the Seventies, and I
hope that these Seventies bring us teeth and eyes, not only in
America but in Britain, which I left forty years ago.

Mr. Newman: Mr. Graves, to what extent can a poet engage in
non-poetic activities without impairing his talent?

Mr. Graves: It's a question of whether he gets cotched.

Mr. Newman: Cotched? oh, 'caught'!

Mr. Graves: Caught, that's right, yes. This world is getting bound
more and more closely in the same system. One takes a job and finds
that one must be loyal to one's organization, even if it means being
disloyal to other allied organizations and to other countries and even,
quite often, to one's relations. I should hate having to decide, if I
found myself part of some organization that was acting in some way
or other against my own personal morality, whether I should stay or
go. Often one can't afford to go because of a sick wife, or a large
family or this, that and the other. So one has to stay; and that's an
ugly thing to face. Innumerable people have to live by what I call
'The Lie': in fact the whole misery of modern life is largely due to
people realizing that they're no longer true to the standards in which
they were brought up. Admittedly some of the standards in which
children get brought up nowadays are pretty permissive.

Mr. Newman: What about political activity for a poet, Mr. Graves?

Mr. Graves: Nothing doing! You may occasionally have to call on
a Prime Minister and read him the riot act. Do you have riot acts in
America?

Mr. Newman: Oh yes.

Mr. Graves: You do? Well, a poet may be forced to go about
things in a pretty strong way. You remember that Shelley talked
about poets being mankind's unacknowledged legislators? So people

have asked me: 'Well, are you a poet?' And I answer: 'Nobody can claim to be a poet; that will be decided only when he is dead.' They say 'You don't deny being one—have you done anything recently in the way of legislation?' I say, 'As a matter of fact, early this year there was a notice in *The Times* that the most important judicial decision made in the past year was in the case of Parsley v. Sweet.' Did you ever hear of Parsley v. Sweet?

Mr. Newman: No, sir.

Mr. Graves: Well, a girl called Stephanie Sweet . . .

Mr. Newman: May I just interrupt for a minute to say that Parsley v. Sweet is in the United States Parsley versus Sweet?

Mr. Graves: Parsley versus Sweet? Very well. Sergeant Parsley was a very pleasant bucolic Oxfordshire policeman who brought a case against Stephanie Sweet, a graduate of Oxford University, who happened to be a college chum of my daughter, but was had up on a charge of managing disorderly premises. In other words, she had rented a country house which, having only about a month of rent left to run and a broken-down car, she lent it to some friends' friends and didn't care what happened there, so long as they paid her the cash. They turned out to be a group of pot-smokers. So Sergeant Parsley made things very unpleasant for Stephanie, poor girl, who found herself in a magistrate's court on a charge of managing a disorderly house: namely a place where drugs were taken. She asked my advice and I told her: 'Do *not* plead guilty!' Her lawyers wanted her to plead guilty, but she took my advice. And I said, 'Okay, I'll help you through, whatever this costs.' The magistrate's court found her guilty, although acknowledging that she didn't know that her subtenants were pot-smokers. She appealed to the Divisional Court. The Divisional Court pronounced her managing of such premises to be an absolute crime, and denied that she could lawfully make any appeal against conviction. When I heard that Stephanie had become an absolute criminal, I said, 'Okay, we'll go to the House of Lords—the supreme Tribunal. It doesn't matter what this costs, you must go through with it.' So we got hold of Rosie Heilbron, Q.C., the smartest woman lawyer in England. Rosie went to the Lord Chief Justice and said: 'Look here, my lord, what's all this about? It is against Common Law to be found guilty of a crime which you do not know is a crime.'

Eventually he considered the case, and five Law Lords to none voted for a change in the law. So now nobody can be convicted of managing a premises unless it can be proved he knew what was happening there and had profited from the knowledge.

Mr. Newman: So you have put through some acknowledged legislation then?

Mr. Graves: It was never acknowledged to me. . . . Sergeant Parsley was very, very much annoyed that his name was given such prominence and that I had called him a very bucolic character. But it had to be done, first of all, by publicizing it in the *Sunday Times*.

Mr. Newman: So you think it's permissible, then, for poets to engage in certain non-poetic activities, when the issue is strong enough?

Mr. Graves: It was a question of justice, which is closely connected with poetry. Stephanie Sweet was a schoolteacher, and she had been sent a letter from the Minister of Education warning her that she must not teach again until she'd been to a head-shrinker. As stupid as that!

Mr. Newman: Mr. Graves, let's take a larger subject. Some American poets, many American poets, many American artists of various kinds, are deeply involved in politics in the United States— very largely, I think, because of the war in Vietnam. Is that likely to affect them—affect their work—do you think?

Mr. Graves: If you protest against the war in Vietnam, you've got to realize what you're protesting against. Who had broken what moral law? It's not enough to say 'I don't like war.' Nobody likes modern war. The important question is: who is doing what? About a ton of American bombs is supposed to have been dropped every twenty yards throughout Vietnam. Has it? A lot of cruel and con- scienceless things have been done, but how do we know that all those many bombs have been dropped? Who is making the money out of their manufacture? Did all those bombs really exist? There are a lot of questions to ask. When the American forces cleared out of France, they found that the enormous pile-up of bombs that they had been asked to remove simply weren't there—and the discrepancy was never explained.

Mr. Newman: But these bombs, if they had been dropped in Vietnam, had presumably exploded—so they would not be still recoverable?

Mr. Graves: No. But on the other hand, if all that are claimed had been dropped and all had exploded, there wouldn't be any Vietnam left. It's difficult to know where you are, you see. One knows—I've heard all about the officers' rest camps in Singapore. I had an English girl-friend who took a good look at one. . . . Well, as people say, 'Isn't it just too bad?' And people who protest against war naturally want to know who makes the money and who is doing what. Strictly speaking, it isn't even a war. War hasn't yet been declared and never will be, because that would bind the U.S.A. to keep to the letter of the Quadripartite Pact which forbids killing of civilians, poisoning of soil and water, and other uncivilized tricks. It's officially called a 'police action'.

Mr. Newman: What do you think is the responsibility of a poet? Is he, perhaps, as you earlier quoted from Shelley, an 'unacknowledged legislator'? In your own case, you were in uniform for a long time in World War I, and had a very terrible war.

Mr. Graves: It was a nice clean war.

Mr. Newman: Clean?

Mr. Graves: Well, until almost half-way through. Then it became anybody's war because it started getting dirty.

Mr. Newman: The question I'm leading up to is: since the conduct of nations and the activity of nations can bring about wars, to what extent . . .

Mr. Graves: Police actions, please! There's not been a war declared for the last twenty years.

Mr. Newman: My question is: to what extent is anybody—poet or not—entitled to opt out of public activity and out of the activity by which government policies are made? Whether you call them wars or police actions or whatever. How do you justify a private withdrawal from political life?

Mr. Graves: The English tradition of poetic morality, such as it is, comes through the Norman French, from the Welsh, and eventually from the Irish. And curiously enough, the Irish poetic morality was very much dependent on the East, because Ireland got its priests not from Rome but from home, and they were responsible only to the Patriarch of Antioch. But never mind that! Any evasion of sworn international pacts—such as that of making war, and breaking all its rules, and saying this is merely a police action . . . it simply would be unpatriotic to support a government that cannot keep its oath.

Mr. Newman: Have we got off the track? Or I . . .

Mr. Graves: Perhaps we're both off the track. So this morality—which I claim to be English, though it can be traced back through Ireland to the east—implies that nobody, whatever happens, must be allowed to act against his own conscience. And that a poet must denounce falsity wherever denunciation is called for. But it remains a purely personal act. It's no good waving flags, fifty abreast and shouting: 'We don't like war' That's not practical. One must show who's been cheating, who's been lying, who's been making the money in what unjust business. And the poet must pin-point it. . . . If everybody acted poetically there wouldn't be any more nonsense. Sometimes a poet can take action.

Mr. Newman: Mr. Graves, you said earlier in this interview that you no longer fear death, because you have already once officially died.

Mr. Graves: Yes, and so have a lot of other people. But would you like to know how crazy I am? (*Mr. Newman laughs*) Well, I have come to agree with my advanced mathematic friends who now agree that time is only a convenience, having no absolute sense. So when one does any real thinking—take, for instance, Rowan Hamilton, the young Irish mathematician who invented Quaternions back in 1842. . . . He was strolling across Phoenix Park, Dublin when suddenly this important formula came to his head. He happened to have a penknife with him, and cut the formula in stone on the bridge across the Liffey, now called Quaternion Bridge. Quaternions are among the chief mathematic props in nuclear physics. How can one dart nearly a hundred years ahead of time?

The simple answer is, time doesn't exist. People often plead, 'It was not my fault'—blaming their parents for giving them a difficult childhood, and so on. I take sole responsibility for having been born. My parents never chose me, because they knew nothing about me and had no idea which of their own genes I'd choose, what I'd look like, what sort of life I'd live. . . . Then who *did* know? It's no good saying 'God' because God is surely a mere question mark? So I say: 'I arranged it all myself!' Now, to make yourself responsible for your

entire life, and all your stupidities, successes, ill luck, joys and suffer-
ings, puts you in a very strong position, because you can blame
nobody else. But the question arises: when were these decisions
taken? Obviously you didn't exist *before* your time, although you can
mentally go back in time and forward in time, which is quite a common experience among clairvoyants. Then precisely when did I make
myself? . . . At the moment of my death.

Mr. Newman: At the moment of your death?

Mr. Graves: Why not? That's the only time when one's life is
complete. And of course, when you're dying, your whole past life is
said to come flooding in with precise memories. Very well! That gives
you a neat package all tied up. Yet it has not yet happened, and from
the point of view of people living in other solar systems it won't
happen until millions of years hence.

Mr. Newman: You had an experience happily denied to the vast
majority of people. You were . . .

Mr. Graves: Why 'happily'? Scores of my friends got killed.

Mr. Newman: I say 'happily' because—because you were badly
wounded.

Mr. Graves: Listen, I'm seventy-five, and I'll still run you a hundred yards. No? you won't?

Mr. Newman: Your own attitude to time and to what comes after,
happens to be expressed in a poem that I was going to ask you to
read. It expresses your view of whether a poet should think about
what honours are coming his way.

Mr. Graves: Well, fame can be very useful if you're crossing a
frontier and you want to take something questionable through the
Customs. Otherwise, it can be an awful bore.

Mr. Newman: Well, you helped us get some equipment into
Spain for recording this program . . .

Mr. Graves: That's exactly it. Well, this poem? Oh, yes, if you
insist:

> To evoke posterity
> Is to weep on your own grave,
> Ventriloquizing for the unborn:
> 'Would you were present in flesh, hero!
> What wreaths and junketings!'

And the punishment is fixed:
To be found fully ancestral,
To be cast in bronze for a city square,
To dribble green in times of rain
And stain the pedestal.

Spiders in the spread beard;
A life proverbial
On clergy lips a-cackle;
Eponymous institutes,
Their luckless architecture.

. . . in case you or anybody doesn't know what 'eponymous' means,
it's a four-bit word. Vanderbilt . . .

Mr. Newman: Vanderbilt University . . .

Mr. Graves: Vanderbilt University is an eponymous institution; so
is Duke University. And there are a whole lot of other *eponymia*
around, such as Kennedy Airport—it used to be Idlewild, when I
knew it first. Now it's an eponymous institution.

Two more dates of life and birth
For the hour of special study
From which all boys and girls of mettle
Twice a week play truant
And worn excuses try.

It has some more verses; let's forget about them. What else did you
want to say?

Mr. Newman: I'd like you, if you would, to read *Spite of Mirrors.*

Mr. Graves: Oh, this is . . .

Mr. Newman: Malcolm Muggeridge asked you whether the
women to whom your poems were written were real or imaginary?

Mr. Graves: Yes.

Mr. Newman: Well, this is certainly a poem about a woman; I
don't know whether real or imaginary . . .

Mr. Graves: Yes, well—she was partly Mexican, partly Basque
and partly Italian.

O what astonishment if you
Could see yourself as others do,
Foiling the mirror's wilful spite
That shows your left cheek as the right

And shifts your lovely crooked smile
To the wrong corner! But meanwhile
Lakes, pools and puddles all agree
(Bound in a vast conspiracy)
To reflect only your stern look
Designed for peering in a book—
No easy laugh, no glint of rage,
No thoughts in passionate pilgrimage,
Nor start of guilt, nor rising fear,
Nor premonition of a tear.

And how, with mirrors, can you keep
Watch on your eyelids closed in sleep?
How judge which profile to bestow
On a new coin or cameo?
How, from two steps behind you, stare
At your firm nape discovered bare
Of ringlets as you bend and reach
Transparent pebbles from the beach?
Love, if you long for a surprise
Of self-discernment, hold my eyes
And plunge deep down in them to see
Sights never long withheld from me.

I didn't read that very well. Never mind. It was well-intended.

Mr. Newman: Mr. Graves, are you writing songs now?

Mr. Graves: Am I writing songs? Yes. I was asked the other day to
write a carol for *The New York Times*, and thought, 'That's a silly
thing to do', and then I . . . you see, I now spend a lot of my time
picking up olives. It's the season, and picking is very good for the
back, and keeps your fingers greasy. Also it keeps your mind working, because half the time you don't have to think. And—what was I
talking about?

Mr. Newman: You were talking about writing a song.

Mr. Graves: Yes. So I found myself writing a carol as I was picking
olives. And—I don't know how long other people are going to write
carols. Carol-making is rather an out of date job. Wait a moment.
Yes, here it is.

Mr. Newman: I don't believe it, but . . . (*laughs*)

Mr. Graves:

Shepherds armed with staff and sling,

Ranged along a steep hillside,
Watch for their anointed King
    By all prophets prophesied—
Sing patience, patience,
Only still have patience!

Hour by hour they scrutinize
    Comet, planet, planet, star,
Till the oldest shepherd sighs:
    'I am frail and he is far.'
Sing patience etc.

'Born, they say, a happy child;
    Grown, a man of grief to be,
From all careless joys exiled,
    Rooted in eternity.'
Sing patience etc.

Then another shepherd said:
    'Yonder lights are Bethlehem;
There young David raised his head
    Destined for the diadem.'
Sing patience etc.

Cried the youngest shepherd: 'There
    Our Redeemer comes tonight,
Comes with starlight on his hair,
    With his brow exceeding bright,'
Sing patience etc.

'Sacrifice no lamb nor kid,
    Let such foolish fashions pass;
In a manger find him hid,
    Breathed upon by ox and ass.'
Sing patience etc.

'Dance for him and laugh and sing,
    Watch him mercifully smile,
Dance although tomorrow bring
    Every plague that plagued the Nile!'
Sing patience, patience,
Only still have patience!

Well, now, that is old-fashioned, isn't it? But it takes a great deal of
patience to write it nowadays.

Mr. Newman: And what about the music?

Mr. Graves: I didn't write the music. I've only once written music for a song, and then the words were by someone else. There's often melody at the back of one's head, but the control of words in a song is an astonishing feat, because one must consider the music and the singer at the same time. Besides, the song is incomplete without the music, and the music is incomplete without the song. The two best English song-writers, Dowland and Campion, both wrote their own words to their own music, so that they really went together.

Mr. Newman: Mr. Graves, about poetry: children are exposed to poetry almost as soon as they go to school. But very little poetry seems to remain in the lives of ordinary people. As you have said, it's generally accepted that it's almost impossible for a poet to support himself by writing poetry. Why has poetry faded from the lives of ordinary people, in the so-called advanced countries?

Mr. Graves: It's a matter of climate, physical and moral. Very few poets have written poems in cities, probably because the ancient poetic tradition is closely bound up with trees, fruits, flowers and stars. City-dwellers seldom see any stars: they get blotted out by the polluted sky. Too many tourists come here to Majorca and ask me 'What tree is that?' They don't know the difference between an elm and a birch. They have often never seen orange trees, and when they see oranges growing on mine they plead: 'Oh, may I pick an orange off a tree?' It's sad.

Mr. Newman: Is technological advance destructive of poetry? Is it a bad thing for poetry that we have landed men on the moon?

Mr. Graves: Between you and me, it's the most shocking thing that's ever happened, since Alexander the Great cut the Gordian Knot—when was it?—in about 336 or 334? The Gordian knot? Well, it was a particularly magical knot that was tied on an oxcart at Gordium in Asia Minor. It had been prophesied that whoever could undo the knot, would be Lord of Asia. Alexander fiddled about for hours, but couldn't untie it. The real point about that knot was that it spelt out a holy name in knot-language. You will find examples of knot-language on ancient Irish arabesques and the British Druids used to exchange messages in knot-language. . . . But Alexander was no Druid and couldn't be bothered to study their mysteries. So he took his dagger and cut the knot right across. This was his studied contempt for all religious secrets, and one of the worst moments in history. . . . Alexander went out East and won great victories, but soon came back and drank himself to death. His own country fell to pieces, too. Everything fell to pieces.

Mr. Newman: What you're saying then, Mr. Graves, is that we should allow some mystery to survive.

Mr. Graves: Mystery cannot help surviving. But the point is that once one starts publicizing a mystery, one is heavily punished. I don't mean you personally, Mr. Newman, because I'm sure you wouldn't.

Mr. Newman: Thank you very much.

Mr. Graves: You have only put yourself in the position of asking questions; and put me in the embarrassing position of trying to give you answers.

Mr. Newman: Yes, sir. And thank you for the answers, Mr. Graves.

In Robert Graves's Olive Grove

Gábor Devecseri/1970

From *The New Hungarian Quarterly*, 2 (Winter 1970), 73-82.
Reprinted by permission.

A man is holding on to a cliff beetling over the sea; with his back and nape aslant, parallel with the cliff face, he leans out over the water; when he reaches a rock which allows him to let go his hold, he turns, stands erect and the next moment he dives—just about from first-floor height—into the water. He is seventy-four.

Twenty energetic strokes take him to the shore. He puts his impossibly broad-brimmed straw hat back on his greying hair—hair which stubbornly resists the comb, but is now smoothed down by the brine. Happy, an erect six-feet figure, he stops for a few seconds here and there at small groups of people basking in the sun on the seaweed carpet; a quick word and he is gone—skipping over the boulders and the slope at a brisk trot heading for Deyá, his "desk." For forty years now he has gone through the same routine day after day. Downhill, straining a little, one can just keep up with his walking tempo; uphill hardly anyone is his match.

His wife Beryl had written to Klári and me before our departure. She wrote that if we went down to the bay in Robert's company, the half-hour distance would be much shorter because "Robert walks fast." We now just learnt how fast. So fast that talking on the way is only possible in snatches. But also so fast that if any exciting topic comes up—that is, one exciting for *him*, which on account of his contagious enjoyment becomes stimulating for *every* one of his talking or listening companions the company must stop and sit down on one of the sunlit rocks among the sparsely-growing olives. You feel grateful. For however overwhelming the Graves' inexhaustible hospitality, the natural environment, and the objects and people around may be, the most enviable and thrilling of all are the conversations that we are lucky enough to have with Graves himself.

It soon becomes apparent that this could not happen as often as one could wish, for what really concerns him is making a compost of his own invention out of fruit-rinds, cheeseparings and flowers that have done their turn, as well as all manner of organic matter mixed, sweated and matured; this, and knocking down walnuts; a close third, amongst other household chores, is washing-up which he never lets anyone else do. To be fair, the guests can always do the drying if they wish. The water drips away from the dishes into a hole in the wash-bowl into which a couple of centuries ago the Devil is said to have vanished from a Mallorcan maiden—since then canonized.

Guests are also welcome to help with the knocking down of walnuts. But this again is hardly the best opportunity for conversation. Graves motioned to me to climb the tree and have a go. I am no longer the right age. Graves, twenty-two years my senior, was up and away into the tree before you could say Jack Robinson, wielding a six-foot long stick and standing amidst the branches above his orchard and kitchen garden. From there he could survey the whole of Deyá as far as the beach and the terraced, rock-strewn pine and olive groves on either side; but he doesn't look around, being busy concentrating on his walnuts. He is delighted with finding the big ones; still more with the rotted black ones for he can put those in the compost at once.

Shortly after our return home to Budapest an engaging woman reporter asked me if one could say Graves lived so bucolically because he had studied the ancients so closely? I could only say what my heart and experience had taught me, that I did not think so; that in fact I believed the contrary to be true. That is to say, his constant, first-hand contact with life and the world around him is also responsible for his ability to capture and to bring into the present some of the great men and women of the ancient world. He knows their Age, moves familiarly among their objects and within their landscape. He all but offers them the salad of his own making; what he certainly offers them are his questions.

When he sits amidst his guests on the lawn in the garden he carves chicken, pours wine, disappears for a while to write—only to reappear again suddenly just as newer and newer guests come on the scene unannounced. He now emerges from the alcove adjoining the kitchen, pushing aside the straw curtain that does for a door, or from the French window opening straight into the garden from the house,

now apparently popping out of the air; "this is Klára, this is Gábor,
this is Frank," says Graves; "this is Alice, this is Bruce," says Frank,
no longer a stranger, a few seconds later. And we resume the conversation. That is we guests do, for Graves is now coming back from the
house with an Etruscan statuette in his hand asking whether we
thought it was Etruscan because he did. He praises us since we
agree. "Well-done", he says, and is gone again to write something,
apparently inside, but we continue to hear of him out here in the
world represented now by this piece of lawn and the air above it, for,
says David a young author whom we have met meanwhile as well as
his blond wife ("This is Ann, this is Klára") for, says David, Robert
has written a beautiful poem about the pyramids. Oh yes, says Frank
too, they know Robert's idea about the pyramids where they vainly
looked for the body of Pharoah's sister-wife because they do not
know and do not want to know that there is another one under each
pyramid: "Like the mirror-image of a tree reflected in the water?"—
"That's right!"—And Frank and David compete with each other explaining it to us under the orange trees, on the lawn near the garage
by the highway lined by plots of carob- and fig-trees and cacti. They
even get out pencil and paper building the pyramid, as it were,
according to Grave' notion claiming the rank of a discovery, with the
feminine pyramid under it; and in the evening Graves drew it in perspective in the way the Egyptians would have been unable to draw it,
and under it the way they did draw it, that is to say, in the form of
Solomon's seal known as David's star, as two interpenetrating tri-
angles with their apices up and down; the seal bears witness.

> Under each pyramid lies inverted
> Its twin, the sister-bride to Pharoah,
> And so Solomon's seal bears witness.
> ("Solomon's Seal")

Beryl, the always smiling lady of the house, and the ever-bantering
and good-humoured Catherine, the poet's daughter from an earlier
marriage (the widow of an atomic physicist) and her charming mathematician daughter; also Stephanie, resembling the Egyptians' cat
goddess, the latter's friend, who has long been attached to the family
and Maria, the Mallorcan housekeeper, and the intermittently present
guests—well, they have all long got used to the poet's periodic

disappearances. The three Abyssinian cats—walking across the table from time to time—are not at all surprised when the host jumps up to go and fetch an object that has just been mentioned and returns from his study holding it aloft and obligingly telling its story. Then he pours some of the 1856 Tokay grown in France which, he explains, a follower of Prince Rákóczi introduced in his adopted country; this too has its own story. But a story just begun may end abruptly because he will interrupt his own sentences if something occurs to him—and it always does—and he is already on his feet again to fetch the thing or clipping or whatever it may be that must be seen or touched to appreciate the story. One of the clippings is a series of articles with pictures from the colour supplement of the *Sunday Times* telling of the thousand men and women "who made the twentieth century." "The only thing that annoys me," he says laughing, "is that, thanks to this letter 'G', I appear on the same page with Goebbels and Goering." But most of the things he shows are hand-made objects. He recently told a newspaper reporter that the fewer objects in one's study that were not made by hand, the better, for that was the secret of creative work. Of course there were books there, but a fair few of them were hand-printed in Majorca, some by Graves himself. Indeed Beryl showed us some of them, some were even single-copy editions of volumes of poetry printed in Deya. The objects were present everywhere illustrating the stories, intruding and interrupting and breaking them up. The eventless events of the day always complimented something urgent to do, either in the garden or some sunbathing-cum-mythological exegesis that could not be postponed.

Should life be work or enjoyment? Graves has long answered this recurrent question by his deeds. He answers it by both finding inexhaustible pleasure in his work on the one hand, and by making his greatest or smallest enjoyment alike enrich and invigorate his work on the other. Every true artist does the same. But perhaps nobody has done so with the same visible joy, with the signs of contentment so unmistakable in his quiet energy. So, by being aware of the fact that life in all its details is important, and by thinking that everybody feels, or should feel, the same way about the world, his own self and his own life, the poet is also ready to put the affairs of the world in order in the company of anyone—even though he has just met him for the first time.

Nothing could make clearer that he is involved with everybody, and yet with a separate significance, than the two stanzas of his "All except Hannibal". In this poem he tells us the instruction which Hannibal gave his soldiers when they were menaced by cold at night: let each man sit on the knees of another and warm each other to weather out the night. They all did as told—

> All except Hannibal himself, who chose
> His private tree-stump—he was one of those!

This is the kind of man he, the poet, is. He warms everybody. But he also needs to be on his own. More than that, he has the power to do so, being a man who raises everybody up to become his peer and companion, never renouncing his fellow-men, yet always being aware of his own separate place. Incidentally, it is interesting that one can put one's finger on the location, as it were, of subjective poetry in these lines. For, apart from the little story being raised to a higher level of reality by being related in verse, the only phrase expressing the poet's position is "he was one of those." It is the statement in which these lines culminate and gives the whole poem its *raison d'être*. Robert Graves—once again at table—lifting his hand, just about flagging with it, reminds me to remember: the story is true. One might even smile hearing this. Wouldn't these lines be true even if no historian had recorded the event which Graves moulded into his verse by retelling it. His gesture told me: he thought no. Graves, and I consider this part of the essence of his verse is not proud of having thought of something, but of having discovered it.

In Deya Graves is present everywhere even where he is not, and even when he is not. And not simply because he makes his entrances quite as unexpectedly as he makes his sudden exits, but also because the landscape which impregnates his verse has itself, for those who know it, become impregnated by his verse. The life at Deya, in flagrant contradiction to his oft-repeated statement (to be found also in his books on Majorca) which he gives as an answer to those who asked him to tell something about *his Deya*.

"It's not mine, it's theirs."

It is in fact his, just because he knows and lets others know that it belongs to "them". That is, those people who received him and live around him, whose dignity he respects and who respect his, the peasants, clerks, shopkeepers and fishermen, the olive- and fig-

growers—the Mallorcan gentlemen. All those who—we saw it at
Palma—prevent him from crossing a street until he has had three or
four impromptu conversations right in the middle of the road. And
these people—who include the lovers of his poetry as well as those
who only know that he is one of the Mallorcan gentlemen—have all
slowly walked into his work. Indirectly of course, but certainly. In
much the same manner as the people, objects and events of the
environment, also get into such things, as the work of that princess
heroine contemplating an epic poem (as Odyssey-components) as an
epic ingredient in Graves' novel *Homer's Daughter;* this is a story of
adventure on the surface but is, in fact, a treatise about the nature of
collecting, sorting and organizing the material for any creation about
the creative process. None of these people are shown in his or her
place and function in real life; but all of them in that role which he or
she suggested or made possible. The creator moves them with his
kaleidoscope-turning activity—also unconsciously!—and with his ka-
leidoscope-arresting ability he makes the picture final and no longer
movable at the particular moment when it meets and becomes one
with his idea. This is how Deya streams into Graves works. And just
as he spreads Deya as an olive-green coverlet on the world, the
whole world he created with his poetry covered Deya before our
eyes.

It also includes his son William in whose Deya hotel and its garden
we were first introduced to the delicious meat and fish (made to our
choice as it was), being cooked and roasted in the open air. It includes also Williams's slim Spanish wife and their dreamy-eyed three-
year-old boy. And their guests who, up to then, unknown to the poet,
came to him to say thanks after ten, twenty, forty years for the joyful
experience his works had given them.

It also extends to Bert Morton, the goateed poet of quiet manners
and to Vida, the long-standing resident of Deya, who has written a
guide-book on Majorca and is the great-great-granddaughter of a
Hungarian Jew who was an officer in the 1848 War of Independence.
These two invited us for an evening conversation we shall long
remember. We agreed on everything except bull-fights. A bull was
naturally disposed that way, it was excitable and aggressive, said
Morton. We on the other hand did not know of any bull who had
volunteered to take part in a *corrida.*

And it extends also to the charming couple, physicians both, to

whose two bright little boys Graves, seventy years their senior, is
already plain "Robert".

To David and Ann with whom at sunset on the last day at Deya we
went round, up and down, amidst thorns, flowers, orange groves,
between brooks winding their way through gutters on either side of
the modern motorway, in the dales and woodlands above Deya and
Soller, till we reached their small farmstead. Both of them gave us
their dietary precepts for a lifetime, carefully writing down for us
mankind-redeeming facts from a cookery-book. Leaving the farm
Ann accompanied us a little way. You must visit us in Budapest, we
said to her. She hoped to be able to make it.

"That's not enough. Promise."

"I hope to," she said emphatically, with an angelic smile raising her
arms like wings in jocose token of a vow.

There was a vast number of olives in Deya. With a little exaggera-
tion I could say: under each of them there sits a poet. The group of
American undergraduates on a half-year visit to Deya call themselves
"creative writers." Graves gave them a lecture in an olive grove near
his house. He lectured to them about writing, talking to them,
walking in front of the audience scattered on rocks, clumps of grass,
felled tree-trunks, taking-off and putting on, and fingering his hat, in
mid-sentence ramifying in all directions from the centre of a main
clause, and also instructing them how *not* to write; a schoolboyish
bantering smile and the blue flash of his eyes signal the more sarcastic
of his remarks. Close to them all and yet aloof. Hannibal on his
stump apart. Or still more the Ibycus of his "Ibycus in Samos."

> The women of Samos are lost in love for me:
> Nag their men, neglect their looms,
> And sent me secret missives, to my sorrow.
>
> Who here can blame me if I alone am poet,
> If none other has dared to accept the fate
> Of death and again death in the Muse's house?
>
> Or who can blame me if my hair crackles
> Like thorns under a pot, if my eyes flash
> As it were sheets of summer lightning?

We discovered this lightning later in the eyes of Catherine, his
daughter, whenever she corrected something in our English, apologiz-

ing each time. The summer flash of lightning in her eyes indicated that she nonetheless hoped she had teased us a little and asked forgiveness for that hope of hers.

From time to time a wave of laughter rolled out from the group of "creative writers" towards Robert, only to give way the next moment to engrossed attention, and then gain to expectant curiosity. One of the listeners, the lithe and charming Ellen whom we had met four years earlier at Spoleto when she was still dancing with the American Ballet—but who has since turned writer and illustrator of children's books—she complains down at the bay on unproductive days that she has not written anything yet that morning—she holds a ballpoint pen in suspense, then stops despairingly: you either take notes or listen to Graves' rhapsodic and at the same time strongly concentrated lectures.

There on the hillside, above a valley variegated by the threads of paths meandering through the orange, lemon and fig-tree covered slopes, is the cottage inhabited by Bruce and his wife, Alice, which although it looks like a little hovel on the outside is comfortable and attractive inside. We sit down in the terrace-garden and we still sit there. It is always six o'clock just like at the tea-table of the March Hare, the Dormouse and the Hatter. Only it is not Alice who comes a-visiting here, for here she is at home. She is also an artist following the methods of *Homer's Daughter* in her drawings: she has illustrated an enchanting children's book by Robert. She immortalized her husband Bruce (who is gentle in the day but is inclined to be excitable if ever he should drink a drop too much in the evening) as a hardbitten palace guard. It's not Alice who comes for a visit, but all the world and his wife; the Spanish poet, the American ex-advertising man, now a professor of Creative Writing, the Finnish beat musician all drop in, drink red wine, eat green and black olives, tell their latest stories to those who could not have heard any of the older ones, seeing the story-teller for the first time. They keep coming and going, hanging around leisurely. It is an impromptu Round-Table conference here above the valley as if, above the world, one could wish the world were as peaceful as the valley below. "What we hear about your country," says a sympathetic English film-director with an air of natural impartiality, "must be pretty false?" "Yes," I answered, "just as much as ours is gappy about yours." The conversation is mainly

about the life and position of artists in Hungary and how the opera is
not a doomed artistic form in our country. Calypso's ambassadors
now arrive, an English author and composer and his Italian wife who
live in Malta; the man wears a ring inscribed Gozo, Calypso's Ogygie.
"Why choose to live just there?" The answer is not romantic, it is
because of income-tax, the cause which sends many an English artist
on a latter-day Odyssey. If they stayed at home most of their income
would go on taxation, that's why he and his wife live

> far from his home on a sea-girt isle: 'tis the
> navel of ocean.
> (transl. H. B. Cotterill)

The afternoon wears on. Ronnie, the poet asks us to go and see
his house, too, a little further up on the hill. He is English with an
Irish background, his wife is Icelandic, their first child born in Athens,
the second in Majorca. And this is why he is learning Mallorcan now.
We had already had a foretaste in the Graves' home of the extent to
which Mallorcan differs from Castillian. Maria the maid had spoken a
few Mallorcan words and was surprised that we understood them. Of
course we did—just as four years before we had been able to make
out the notes written by our Sardinian-born host in Spoleto: just as
the Sard idiom differs from Italian by preferring certain classical Latin
words, so Mallorcan differs from Castillian.

Such high esteem for women emanates from Graves's works as can
only follow from judging woman to be at least the equal of man. This
applies even to the negative women characters. An example of this is
a sentence from his I, Claudius, which I have liked best ever since my
school day, " . . . now that Rome has been ungrateful and mad
enough to allow my blackguardly son to put me on the shelf, and
insult me—me, can you imagine it, perhaps the greatest ruler the
world has ever known . . . " Another example is Graves' view that
poetry is always attached to the Muse, to the Muses. And the crowning example of this view is The White Goddess. He related the story
of his best-loved book the previous night, in a beautiful house, much
higher up-hill than Ronnie's nicely furnished cottage (which had been
built by Ronnie and his wife with their own hands) in one of the
houses he uses to put his guests up. He told us that he had offered

this book about Celtic beliefs, the Irish tree-alphabet and the mysteries of poetry to a number of publishers without success. His own publisher, who bought unseen anything he had written or just planned, had refused to consider this strange book for publication. Shortly after this the publisher died. Graves took his MS to another publisher who rejected it and also died almost immediately. The third publisher not only did not want to hear of the publication of the book but said it was the most monstrous rubbish he had ever read. A few days later this gentleman was found in his own garden in knickers and brassiére, hanging from a tree. Then came T. S. Eliot, who said that, although he did not like the book, he was willing to publish it since it was a Graves work. He did publish it eventually and lived in good health for a long time afterwards.

"And what could be the cause of this series of deaths?" we wondered.

"The revenge of the White Goddess," the poet said, not wonderingly but in a dry informative tone.

In *The Nazarene Gospel Restored* Graves wrote about everything that pertained to the Jewish traditions in the New Testament; and in *The White Goddess* he wrote everything that was non-Jewish in this same culture, as well as of countless beliefs in demons, in witches, in their workings and in the nature thereof.

"Shh!" Beryl said one evening; Robert mustn't be disturbed now; he is in conference." Gathered round Robert's armchair were four or five men and women, never seen before or since. They had travelled there a long way only to request his expert opinion in some occult matter.

"Yes," Robert said after they had gone, again at the table, "I can surmise a lot of things. Writing *The White Goddess* I hit upon the solution of the Irish secret writing unexpectedly. Genetically if you like. Some time later I was sent an article concerning the subject. It was signed Graves, but it wasn't me. It turned out that it was my grandfather whose concern in the matter was quite unknown to me."

He knew some Hungarian folk-songs in the same hereditary fashion. He had inherited them in a less mysterious way. At the farewell party of the painter couple we all sang in the peasant house—or rather peasant palace—adorned with all kinds of masterpieces of peasant furniture. Klári and myself sang many Hungarian traditional

songs. "Who can sing a Hungarian solider's song?" one of the party
asked. While Klári and I were thinking, Robert suddenly spoke: "I
. . . I think I know one." He knew more. Quite a few. Old Hussar
songs, recruiting tunes, with English words. The way he recited them
revealed much of the unpathetic pathos of his own poetry, glittering
humour and reverential irony. His comical coming down heavily on
the first syllables of English words and his stressing of conjunctions
were accompanied with jerks of his head and smiles, while he
achieved the overall effect through a naive and therefore serious self-
identification. His partaking of the experience while at the same time
looking at it from a distance with well-meaning and appreciative
superiority, and yet also being able to think of the imparting of the
experience as well as enjoying the communication—this was his
performance. But where did he learn all these military songs?

"From Kodály. I learnt them all from the young Kodály in my
boyhood."

"Where?"

"At home. During his tour of England he was the guest of my
father. The words were translated by my father."

The next day he took us back to more mystical things. What did
we say to his visionary deciphering of a Latin inscription? He saw it
simply as a vision, something projected on a wall. I suspect that this
mystical projection on the wall would have had more difficulty
coming about had he not studied Latin texts for many years before.

Beryl took us in the car to Alcudia, on the other side of the island. We
passed through a valley of man-shaped rocks older than man, the
Torrente de Pareis. Each rock a senator in a toga gathered in folds.
The general assembly in the middle of the valley, on its circumfer-
ence elders in twos and threes learning together. "Let the consuls
consider. . . " But they speak this mostly without heads. Arms they
sometimes have, sometimes not. Bodies, feet showing faintly under
the togas; the flow of the rocks folds makes you trace and complete
in the imagination the missing heads and arms, even the thrust of the
head and the gesture of the arm. The pre-human sculptor was de-
cidedly modern. Above the valley a bazaar with the stretched skin of
mountain goats, hard by a centuries old chapel with time-mellowed
immemorial oils of The Way of the Cross. The goat, the scapegoat,
Christ passes in these pictures amidst his snarling immolators and

torturers—much like in that early poem 'In the Wilderness', the scapegoat, beside Jesus—the poet's own self—roams the wilderness. Lower down stands a monastery surrounded by woods, and on an elevation a more than ruinous ruin, not an old building but one deprived of its future, the skeleton of a luxury hotel abandoned (because it was erected in an inaccessible place). Not much later we came to a small inviting pine-wood. Here we stop the car and get out. Walking under the cones and on the carpet of pine-needles what's more natural than that the White Goddess should come to mind? I ask Beryl whether Robert seriously believed that the deaths of all those publishers were the revenge of the White Goddess?

"Read the book and you'll believe it too," replies Beryl almost indignantly at such great incredulity. Then she asked if I thought it likely that *The Nazarene Gospel Restored* and *The White Goddess* should be published in Hungary.

"After all I've heard," I said, "it's absolutely certain. I know the directors of all the publishing houses. Each of them is a real man. They all know how much better they look in a suit than in lingerie."

In Alcudia the red wine we drink at the inn—graced with stuffed birds—tastes exactly like that unique wine we had tasted in Ithaca five years before. The pirates did not roam the seas in those far-off times without fulfilling a useful mission.

And what about the Moorish occupation? It wasn't a bloodless affair either. And yet even that has left beneficial marks all over the place. The waving olive groves for instance on the terraces above the waterfront.

"I don't know what we'd do without the Moors," Beryl said at Lluch Alcari as we descended the terraces cut by the Moors nine hundred years ago, when we were going towards the house in one of the *other* bays where the Graves have their Sunday picnics.

This bay also helped me to understand why Graves had chosen to settle on this side of the island between George Sand's and Chopin's Valdemosa, and the fruit-producing Soller and Lluch Alcari adorned with grapes, ancient Spanish peasant cottages and trees of unfathomable shade, instead of choosing the tourist paradise or a village near Palma in the south. Though I must admit that the taller and more slender senator-rocks on the way in the deep valley of rocks would have certainly been really best complemented by the poet's features.

The farewell picnic took place a Lluch Alcari.

Changing in a straw-hut for the beach; siren-rocks among which the sea has been playing hide-and-seek from time immemorial with its aquatic sculptures appearing right in the same places for millions of years.

Then the vine-trellished old house. The key is with the owner of the farm next door. Graves shakes hands with the man and presses his patriarchal lips on the young woman's cheek.

Once more time stops in the small garden high above the water. This timelessness is Robert's gift emanating from his personality. Leisurely talk, of which he is the natural focus. Everybody has his share of the talking but the subjects are all suggested by him. Now he is talking about names. Catherine means "pure" from the Greek *katharos*. And Klára is its Latin counterpart. Catherine speaks about various weaknesses of the law in Australia; she also mentions the Hungarians living there. In contrast with Robert, who said once before that he had not met an antipathetic Hungarian and said later in Budapest that he had not met a stupid one either—we must certainly consider him lucky—Catherine's view is more balanced, but is still a bit romantic:

"I have known only two kinds of Hungarians: the best and the worst. 'It would be nice,' she turned suddenly to me, "if your wife could stay here for a long time." Then she added politely, "And you, too."

"Do you know what is so great in this house?" asked Lucia, Robert's and Beryl's daughter, some while later in Madrid, where we were the guests of herself and her husband, the young composer Ramon Farran. "It is," she answered her own question, "that we need not sort the garbage."

Into organic and inorganic, that is. As it must be at home, on Majorca, for "Robert's great work," this is how the Mallorcan friends always referred to it—the compost.

She also asked us where we lived in Deya. We told her we stayed in their place. The house in Robert's garden was the home of Ramon and Lucia and their three-year-old daughter, the gay child and serious adult, Natalia.

"And do you know how Robert got to Deya in the first place?"

"Robert, Robert . . . " he was Robert to everyone, to his daughter, to his three-and five-year-old grandchildren; not grandfather or daddy. To the admirers, too, he was not Mr. Graves but a devoutly spoken "Robert"—kings, kings of poetry included, lose their sur-names.

"It happened forty years ago that he wrote his poem "The Legs" about legs hurrying to and fro in the metropolis, each pair bound for some destination, and he did not want to be legs. The next day he left for Deya and has stayed there ever since."

Indeed, one cannot see the highway from Robert's terrace, nor from that of Lucia and Ramon, where we spent so much time. We saw not legs and legs but only heads and heads over the low hedge and those only rarely; sauntering, not hurrying.

On this tiny terrace we worked with Robert's friends, Claribel Alegria, the fiery-eyed South-American poet and her author-hus-band, the infinitely sympathetic Bud Flaco. Together we worked on some lines I had written and dedicated to Robert and Beryl on this very terrace in the remaining tail-end of our farewell afternoon in Deya. The previous night, after listening to Claribel's poems, I had read them aloud in Hungarian, going through them line by line to indicate the line-ends and explaining the words. Now we worked leisurely as on a piece of knitting or doing a cross-word puzzle. Two versions were completed.

Una sola miranda abrazabdola toda:
aceitnuas,
una milión de aceitnuas.
A la distancia el mar con sus frutes-peces
ondulantes;
entre los dos
precipies héraldos proclamando
la infinita hora.

De pie aqui, en esta colina
ante una querida casa
soy una estaca en el camino sin fin
Señalando mi existencia aqui y ahora.

And here is Bud's version a shade more freely translated:

A single glance embraces all:
olives,

perhaps a million olives,
far-off with fidgeting fish-fruit,
the sea, and 'twist the two
precipices proclaiming endless hours.

I stand on a small hill near a beloved house
a stake set in the long, long road,
fixed here midst fish and flowers.

I took his manuscript to Robert and handed it to him. I thought
they would look at it months later. That same evening we found
Robert, Beryl and Catherine standing over the MSS spread on the
table. "This is very nice," said all three of them about Claribel's
version. "And this too," spoke Beryl pointing at Bud's translation.
"But something is missing." "And then there're words in them," said
Robert, "which are too poetic." Then suddenly turning to me he
said:

"Wouldn't you like me to do it?"

I stood by Robert and started to explain the words and the aura of
each of them, forgetting that I was standing next to a magician who
still vividly remembered the recital the previous night. "Get away," he
snapped at me jocosely. I and the others went into the adjoining
room. Scarcely a quarter of an hour later Robert rejoined us waving
two versions—one heavily corrected and one fair copy:

Here I survey all with a single glance:
Green olives in their myriads;
Far off, fruited with moving fish,
The sea; and in between
Tall cliffs recording endless hours.

I stand here in the calm of the morning
Before this beloved house:
A stake marking an endless road
With my own Here and Now.

Now we were all standing above this version. At that moment
Robert, after the last minute, rewrote two—not lines—letters. He
capitalized Here and Now. And with this he raised the whole poem,
not into the realm of pathos but making it more exact, confirming me
in my view about the importance of nuances. To skip lines is the
reader's prerogative. For a writer, while he is working on a poem,
there is not insignificant letter, let alone insignificant words.

How unsuspecting I was!

Who had fondly believed that I would be able to present at least these two stanzas to the novelist of my school days, the poet of my manhood, my host under the leaves of the olives and always under the leaves of universal poetry.

It was he who presented me with my own poem, too.

Playboy Interview: Robert Graves
James McKinley/1970

From *Playboy*, 17 (December 1970), 103-16. Reproduced by Special Permission of *Playboy* Magazine: Copyright © 1970 by *Playboy*.

The long and distinguished career of Robert Graves began where it might well have ended—in the trenches of France in 1915, when a shellburst nearly emasculated him, "clinically killing me." But Graves obviously resurrected himself and, in the intervening 55 years, has become a famous, sometimes notorious poet, critic, translator, mythologizer and commentator on the passing scene. Now 75, Graves spans our century. He has explored almost all its dimensions in his 130-plus published books, moving through it with a prickly, idiosyncratic style inherited partially from his father, an Irish poet, and his mother. a Bavarian gentlewoman fond of Gothic castles and supernatural legends.

Graves first wrote poetry when he was 11 years old; he has never stopped. After returning from World War One, he married his first wife, sired four children and continued writing poems and sociopsychological criticism until he could no longer stand the society that was the core of his criticism. He left England and his personal ties in 1929, and his leavetaking book, "Good-bye to All That," remains both the best description of those troubled times and a characteristically honest self-portrait.

He moved to the then-remote Mediterranean island of Majorca, where he has lived ever since, except during the Spanish Civil War and World War Two, when he returned to Englnd briefly and reluctantly. In 1945, he went back to Majorca with his second and present wife and settled in to raise his second set of four children. Living on his island, Graves has remained far enough from contemporary social and literary whirls to develop startlingly original notions about the way books and people should be. Catholic taste and a penchant for prodigious scholarship have helped him along the way. As a novelist, Graves pioneered the technique of transcribing past events into present-day nomenclature and psychology—a feat he feels comes from a poetic ability to suspend time in the mind. His 1934 novel "I, Claudius" stands as a landmark among historical "reconstructions."

As a critic, he has consistently held out for what he calls the native tradition of English poetry, one rooted in love and dedicated to an exploration of the complicated relationship between men and women. He says, "No individual love, no grass, no birds or animals—that is what makes . . . most modern poems so disastrously dull." He also steadfastly affirms the need for meter and rhyme in poetry, which brings him into headlong collision with nearly every other major contemporary poet. No matter. His gadfly essays have attacked them all, notably Yeats and Eliot, as talented but misled.

Graves's mythological researches have shocked and outraged the academic community but have drawn no conclusive rebuttal. Strongly supporting his hypotheses with evidence "intuited" from history, he has asserted that all true poetry begins in savage, prehistoric matriarchal rites; thus, all poets owe fealty to a cruel, capricious Earth Mother he calls the White Goddess. He has declared that Christ survived the cross and died in his 70s preaching in India and, with equal seriousness, that drinking milk causes homosexuality in some men. He was among the first to claim that hallucinogenic drugs were fundamental to most of the world's great religions and he himself has tripped to "the land of the dead" via magic mushroom; he reports that it was a fine experience because he could see sounds and hear colors. These are desirable qualities for a man who says that Solomon's "Songs of Songs," which he is currently translating is really the account of a wedding ceremony.

Yet with all these accomplishments, Graves has never felt himself anything but a poet. His poetry, he says, is his "spiritual autobiography." He claims he writes all the rest so he can afford to write poems. "Poetry, as I understand it, is written from personal necessity, not for the market. It is made as an oyster makes pearls." Presumably, Graves means out of sand and time, with a generous boost from the private muse he thinks must inform, through love, every poem worth the name. His latest collection of poems celebrates this belief. And many think his efforts have made him the finest love poet of the century. In 1961, he was elected professor of poetry at Oxford and he has won prizes at two Olympic Games for poems, most recently, the

Gold Medal at Mexico City's 1968 contest. Queen Elizabeth II and the American National Poetry Society have also awarded him gold medals for his poetry, though he returned the American one when he found it wasn't really gold.

Iconoclasm marks Graves's every activity. In lectures to college audiences, he mentions the mind-expanding properties of drugs, then informs his listeners only the "priestly" should use them. His polyglot scholarship confounds and annoys strait-laced academicians, though many pick up his ideas for investigation. Charged with sad, deeply felt emotion, his poetry is carefully wrought and elegantly expressed, which perplexes and delights readers accustomed to more modern modes. Even his day-to-day surroundings set him apart. PLAYBOY correspondent Jim McKinley, a friend and neighbor of Graves, conducted this revealing interview in Graves's Majorcan home.

"Though I've known Robert Graves for some time," he writes, "and been to his house often, there still seems an aura of mystery, of special knowledge, around him and his house. Nothng menacing or forbidding, just special. From our mountain village, you walk out toward Graves's house along a narrow road for about a mile. You go between lemon and olive trees, listening to the finches and sheep bells and looking at the Mediterranean. It seems a fitting setting for Graves, with his interest in the ancients. You can't help visualizing him striding along in a tunic. This 75-year-old, six-foot, three-inch man marches the two miles to and from the post office twice a day, at a pace you can't match even though you're 40 years younger. He always wears a hat on these jaunts, a floppy straw or a tam or a Spanish black pull-down thing that looks like a World War One flier's helmet. It sits on a big head—gray-haired, gray-eyed, with a nose crooked from a low rugby tackle and an occasional left hook.

"We talked in his study, in the house he built when he came to the island many years ago with a poet friend named Laura Riding. She is long since gone. Now the room resonates to his soft speech—a Mayfair accent that can't hide the Celtic burr underneath—and to the sounds of Graves's second family, his lovely wife, Beryl, and their children. A white poodle scratches once in a while at the oak door. His youngest son, Tomas, 16, entertains visiting grandchildren and nieces with a guitar. Graves leans back in a handmade rocking chair that squeaks. He wears a loose gray shirt, open at the neck, and, as always, a bright scarf at his throat. Very calm and serene.

"We are surrounded with leather-bound books, wood carvings, all sorts of 'magical objects,' as Graves calls the innumerable stones, rings, icons, glass marbles, feathers and pottery he has accumulated from around the world. The *ambiance* is warm, nearly religious. Before we begin, Graves's wife comes in with tea from Ceylon and home-made bread and the marmalade Robert made from lemons and oranges in their garden. 'I like it tart,' he says. Judging from appearances, Graves is very much the pa-triarch, the country gentleman at home. Yet for most of his artistic life he has sworn allegiance to woman as supreme. The interview began on that note as his wife carried out the tray."

Playboy: Much of your literary work centers on love and morality and the historical roles of the male and female. Do you think the sexual revolution has altered any of these traditional values and relationships?

Graves: If you mean free sex, before and after marriage, it violates the moral principles on which the state was founded. And of course the birth rate will probably go up, despite contraception, and once you have 2.3 births per family instead of 2.0, that sends everything haywire. Then the natural genius of the race for self-preservation calls a halt and the result will be a sharp increase of homosexuality, and also drug taking, some of which may cut down people's lives to the 30s and 40s.

Playboy: Would you explain that?

Graves: What happens when you encourage free sex is that you pervert the natural sexual drive into one of excessive sexuality. This excessive sexuality is then manifest in overpopulation, even beyond the check of contraception. Threatened by disaster through over-population, man probably tends to rein his heterosexual drive. This leaves the instinct for sexuality, made excessive by free love, to find its outlet in homosexuality or drug taking. And, as I said, heavy use of some drugs cuts a person's life span, because the human body is physically debilitated and later destroyed.

Playboy: You view these trends as a result of permissive sexual attitudes?

Graves: To a great extent in cities of the West; and take what's happened in Africa, where there was once widespread emphasis on the sanctity of woman and her role as moral agent. Today, this tribal morality has completely broken down. This is a product of the West, the introduction of Western culture and sexual morality, of missionaries destroying the ancient tribal ways of solving problems, even the population problem. I know of only one place where the old tribal ways are intact and that is in Brazilian jungles, because they are protected by the government. And the most shocking evidence of moral breakdown is in the civilized Western countries.

Two nights ago, I went to a night club in Palma, because some friends of mine were singing there. In the intervals, there was dancing. I hadn't seen dancing for some time, since all the carefree, wild, easy jumping around of the 1950s. But here were couples jigging opposite each other and simulating the sexual act. To me, that was disgustingly public, because I believe the original human instinct, like that of all intelligent beasts, is to perform sexual acts in privacy. But as soon as the ancient taboo on open sex activity—which starts from both natural caution and true affection—is broken down, you develop this cult of obscenity. If anybody had seen this dancing 20 years ago, he'd have either gone and kicked their bottoms or stalked out. The most amazing thing was that these dancers were respectable tourists from the luxury steamship in the harbor.

Playboy: Many would call what you saw symptomatic of a new interpersonal freedom—and your reaction rather prudish.

Graves: Many people have no idea how to separate worthwhile things from stupid, even dangerous things. Such exhibitionism isn't free or good. It comes close to mindless perversion. It signals the end of romantic love, and I don't believe people really want that. I even think that they feel a bit uncomfortable with their new freedom, with the attitude that "anything goes." What freedom do you get by the abandonment of all moral sense and the discovery that you can "get" almost any girl you want by giving her enough drink or drugs?

Playboy: True enough. But does responsible permissiveness, if you'll permit us to use the term, necessarily lead to moral breakdown?

Graves: You must remember the moral nature of permissiveness. Women dictate morals and you cannot separate sex and morality. Historically, it is the woman who must rule and guide in this realm. She is the moral officer and when she is denied this prerogative—as in today's patriarchal society—a moral breakdown follows, because the only moral code a man has is his sense of honor, and few still have that nowadays.

Playboy: Would you explain?

Graves: My explanation lies in history and the changes in societies and cultures which took place centuries ago. You see, before the second millennium B.C., matriarchal peoples controlled the lands in the Middle East and Europe and established a high civilization there. Women ruled. Men were allowed only to have their harpoons, sailing ships, hatchets, slings, and so on. There was no marriage as in the male-dominated societies, where women belong to men. In matriarchal systems, women dictated morality and kept men honorable. A woman had her man for as long as she wanted to and then discarded him. Therefore, all ancestry was traced through the mother: A woman agreed that she had children by a man, but this had absolutely no effect on property, because all lands and houses were held by women. They set up clans that produced needed goods which were exchanged with other clans. But once a clan produced a surplus of nonperishable goods, the barter system broke down. If one clan had too many copper ingots in reserve, or blue beads, or canoes, say, as opposed to vegetables or fruit, these would become a symbol of power. A superfluity of silver and copper was the start of money. That's how world trade and money started.

All of which was very well, but it weakened the centrality of the clans. And when one clan was able to trade with clans outside the tribe, rather than inside, that clan gained power. When the balance was upset and others wanted an equal share of the power from external trade, this led to piracy and then to war by the men who did the trading. Piracy and acts of violence—wars—are a male affair. Under a matriarchy, women would also arm to keep peace within the tribe and on the frontiers. The female aim was life and fertility. But between 2000 and 1000 B.C., the patriarchalist nomads broke in from the deserts and invaded the matriarchal lands. The patriarchalists, who had never had a clan-exchange system and lived from their flocks and herds, were driven west by desiccation. They invaded the matriarchal lands, where they saw the opportunity to gain more goods of symbolic wealth and power. Also, with these male-dominated invaders, we began to develop our picture of the submissive female. The patriarchalists had no need of women for their sacred rites. Women were little use to them except to bear children, sew skins and milk cows. The English word daughter means milkmaid.

Playboy: That's the same sort of male chauvinism men are being accused of today by militant feminists. How do you feel about the tactics of the women's liberationists?

Graves: As soon as women organize themselves in the male way, with societies and memberships and rules, everything goes wrong. For regaining true feminity, the impulse must be a natural woman-to-woman understanding, spontaneous and secret.

Playboy: What do you see as the woman's proper role in our own time? Do we need a change in the attitudes of both sexes?

Graves: Attitudes toward woman have changed a great deal lately but in the wrong direction. The traditional rules were that a man opens a door for a lady, pays for her dinner if they go out together, doesn't force himself on her in any rude way, gives her presents. But the unisex system aims to abolish this relationship, and that's a great pity. The very act of love is a giving by the man to the woman, and the man is the more pleased the greater the sense he gets of her enjoyment. It's very sad today to see old women giving young men presents in order to keep their affection. Women should be limited to the giving of ties and that sort of thing as presents—on birthdays and at Christmas. Anything more destroys the proper relationship of man to woman. I also think that all house property should be in the name of women, not in the name of men, because otherwise they can't be its real managers.

Playboy: Why *should* women be the managers of property?

Graves: Well—to answer a fool according to his folly—that makes a man much more careful about whom he marries. If you marry a woman and give her control over the house you live in, you have to watch your step. Otherwise, after seven or eight marriages, you won't have many houses left.

Playboy: Do you think marriage will continue to exist in its present form?

Graves: I think marriage as an institution will be out in a generation's time. There can still be unwritten contracts between a man and a woman if they want to be together, and no one should disturb them. The woman won't be dependent on the man for providing for children, because the state will be doing that. The present arrangement is what makes women so tyrannous and cross when they have to bear the burden themselves.

Playboy: Without marriage, will women be able to function effectively as men's moral officers?

Graves: Marriage in the real sense is beyond institution. But you find that only in about one case in ten: a man and a woman who keep an enshrined dependence on each other, year after year, which is not simply sex or children. They are defined a real couple. To find real couples is as delightful as it is rare. When a man and his beloved are concerned about each other even when apart, they can, without making a conscious decision, offer love to one another over that distance. They can miraculously create all sorts of strange happenings. These are part of the miracle and they are created by a love axis between a man and a woman. On this love axis they can do amazing things for each other by twisting time and space into a ring—end to end, so that they perceive and control events and emotional states in an apparently impossible way. The lovers exchange radiant messages outside of time and space, often unknowingly.

When I speak of love, of course, I always differentiate between two phases of love. Many people say they are in love, but being *in* love with a person and loving a person are quite different. Being in love will imply a definite sexual or physical attraction which naturally asks to be consummated. But one can love people without any need for sexual or physical attraction. One can love people as if a brother or sister. I have a lot of relationships like that. When we speak of lasting ties between a man and a woman, this means that they seldom get divorced while they are still in love. When they are *in* love—that's the time of the greatest emanations or radiations. The electrical forces are enough to bring on a tropical storm or blow a fuse.

Playboy: Does everyone give off theses radiations?

Graves: Some people don't radiate at all, so they don't really exist, at least not in any noticeable way. If they died, nobody would notice their absence. I don't claim to have any great radiative powers myself. But I know that everything in this room, in which I have lived for so long, has my radiations in it. Most people, through their own emanations, imbue their household property with themselves. For example, my house here, which seems full of spirits, like everything in it. There is practically nothing in this room which isn't handmade—those glasses, pictures, bookshelves, everything. But even things that are machine made can be imbued with your spirit. You can make even a machine part of you. It takes about six months or a year to tame a machine. Until then, it remains inert and sterile. Say a camera which learns to take wonderful photos but which you lose; even if you get another just like it, it will take six to 12 months before it can take your pictures properly. You see, human beings need time to put their spirit into modern machines. And expendability, planned obsolescence, makes this very difficult; things are worn out before we can tame them. Especially cars and musical instruments.

Playboy: You've written that certain places on earth give off mysterious radiations that affect the inhabitants. How?

Graves: There are some sacred places made so by the radiation created by magnetic ores. My village, for example, is a kind of natural amphitheater enclosed by mountains containing iron ore, which makes a magnetic field. Most holy places in the world—holy not by some accident, like a hero dying or being born there—are of this sort. Delphi was a heavily charged holy place.

Playboy: The increasing use of drugs seems related to what you apparently think is a human need to feel some sort of mystical relationship with other people and places, to sense the radiations. How do you feel about drug use?

Graves: Most people use drugs for kicks, without the crucial element of moral responsibility. I have eaten the Mexican magic mushroom myself—but only in a state of grace to explore the ancient paradise of Tlalocán. I have no need or use for meditation. In fact, I wrote a pertinent rhyme the other day:

In a small heap triangular
Our budding Buddha meditates.
Gates of Nirvana stand ajar,

He stares unwinking at the gates.
Brown rice his food, water his drink.
Hey, stop that meditating! Think!

Playboy: How does that poem relate to drug usage?

Graves: There is a sort of false mystic who uses the drug of meditation about nirvana to stop himself from active thinking. You see,
hallucinogens were originally to be used solely for religious purposes
and only in the hands of the priestly elite. In fact, all the big religions
of the world, with the exception of Christianity, which is of late and
mixed origin, derived their ideas of heaven from experiences with a
particular form of mushroom, the *Amanita muscaria*. Its effect is to
deny a sufficient oxygen supply to the brain and thereby set loose
hallucinations. The Indian, the Oceanic, the Mexican, the Greek, the
Sumerian, the Hebrew, the Babylonian and the Vedic religions all
originally had their ideas of heaven produced by this drug.

But let me recall the Greek story of Tantalus, which I think best
illustrates the danger which historically befell mortals, nonreligious
persons, who merely wanted to experiment with this divine ambrosia
for their own pleasure. Tantalus was a mortal who defied the gods by
partaking of the hallucinatory mushroom. Therefore, the gods bound
him up to his neck in water. He was terribly thirsty, but whenever he
lowered his head to drink, the water sank away. And above his head
hung the most beautiful fruits; but when he raised his hand to grasp
them, they also disappeared. This was his punishment for having
eaten the food of the gods and inviting his mortal friends to try it. No
one who is not priestly is entitled to it.

Playboy: So you liken those who take drugs for kicks to Tantalus?

Graves: They will have his punishment. And just as Tantalus was
condemned by the gods never to be able to achieve anything he
desired, few of them will ever reach their maturity or their goals.

Playboy: Are there any circumstances under which you would
condone the use of drugs by people not of a priestly elite?

Graves: Well, I have an idea which might be useful. I think that at
the time Protestants have their confirmations and Jews have their *bar
mitzvahs,* about the age of 14 or 15, children should be isolated and
put under very strict discipline for three weeks. They should be fed
very little and kept away from all distractions. Then they should be
given the sort of treatment one got in the ancient Greek mysteries.

They should be purged and frightened and then given a harmless hallucinogen. While under that, they should be taught the moral rules of life. This was done in the old days at Eleusis. And that is why, in spite of having a ridiculous state religion with seven gods and five goddesses in which nobody believed, there are basic good faith and proper behavior among those so initiated. The priests of Dionysus screened the adepts for three years. Initiates were promised they would go to the paradise they had visited under the drug if they continued in a state of grace. If any had bad visions, this was because they weren't in a state of grace.

Playboy: In their search for mystical experience, their spiritual wanderings and their renunciation of personal property, many of today's hippies have been likened to the early Christians. Do you see any similarity?

Graves: The hippie culture is wholly unreligious; they have no god and no prophet. Yet some of its aspects can be admired in a way. For example, a man and his "family," a good-sized commune of 20, came here after they were chucked out of Ibiza for hashish. I rather liked him. He was a big Negro who had spent five years in a Mexican jail, but the experience hadn't spoiled him. Instead, it had made a man of him. Here he at once appropriated my neighbor's flute and he tried to get my guitar, but I liked him anyway—he had a great conscientiousness about his family and there was no nonsense about him. He was a strong man and a good man. He could love.

Playboy: Are those characteristics—strength, responsibility, love— what make a man good, as far as you're concerned?

Graves: In my opinion, if a man hasn't got honor, he's worth absolutely nothing. And, unfortunately, too many people are tricked out of their honor by some means or other, like having to obey a boss. If he tells them to do things they know are wrong and they do them, they have lost their honor.

Playboy: How do you define honor?

Graves: Honor is the sense of your correct relation to your imme- diate surroundings, including your fellow workers. It's your duty to your clan or crowd, if you belong to one. Yet few of us belong to a real clan now that tribal systems have been dispersed. We're just reckoned to belong to some sort of industrial or agricultural complex. The hippies, of course, have their clans and remain true to them.

Even thieves, until recently, had a strong sense of honor among themselves. Their honor allowed them to rob other people but not within their clan.

Playboy: At least for thieves, that would seem to be less honor than professional courtesy.

Graves: The difference is small but indicative. I was here the other day when a young Californian wandered in and started reading my letters. I said, "Here, what are you doing?" He replied, "Isn't that an interesting remark?" and pointed to a letter. Whereupon I said, "Listen, if this were England, I would have taken you by the neck and kicked you out of the room, but as you come from a place where the traditions of manners and privacy are seldom preserved, where people wander through each other's houses, I must only say that one doesn't do that in my house." He stopped and never did it again.

Playboy: Can you generalize about people's behavior from this one incident?

Graves: Well, at least I believe people instinctively know what is right and wrong. When you don't realize your behavior is wrong, you deceive yourself. That's a severe punishment, both for you and for the one you've wronged.

Playboy: Hemingway once remarked that what is moral is what you feel good after and what is immoral is what you feel bad after. Would you agree with that?

Graves: It's rather an oversimplification. I never really trusted Hemingway.

Playboy: Would you agree, then, with Edmund Burke that "all that is necessary for the forces of evil to prevail is that enough good men do nothing"?

Graves: That's a very wise remark. But, of course, if good men do nothing, they aren't good men. Good is a positive action—like behaving well in someone's home. But I'm afraid there aren't enough good men acting positively today. That's why I don't think anything can be done for the world the way it is at the moment, because the people at the top are so scared of the people below who are able to destroy them. The police forces all over the world and, to some extent, the soldiers have been so infiltrated with evil elements that no one trusts anybody. Nothing can be done except for good people to avoid evil people and avoid being closely involved in the big lie.

Playboy: What's the big lie?

Graves: It's money, which originated when the clans began bartering item for item. It all started with interclan exchange of love gifts. Yet, from this sense of mutual dependence, kindness and generosity, there arose greed, cunning, usury. Still, until recently, it consisted of something you could at least see: gold and silver. Now there is no money left. Money today is all checks, promises. Being promises, it is also lies. And people get caught in the lie and can't get out. The evil people are the ones who worship money. They are held back by no morality, not even the ordinary restraints that are found in any organized religion such as Catholicism or Protestantism or Judaism. The very evil are in control. The number of workers who are free from obedience to money is extremely small. It's practically impossible to be free from it, because money means power and our world is power oriented.

Playboy: Do you think young people realize the danger and will do something about this evil in high places?

Graves: Well, I'm hopeful that they will. They seem to be reaching back for suprarational knowledge.

Playboy: How can suprarational knowledge solve the world's problems?

Graves: Because of their interest in occult powers, the young are looking for answers beyond the computer—which was the middle generation's answer. They are trying to control the emanations of our human condition, the sources of thought which extend forward and backward through time, to get direct experience and understanding. A new interest in the occult is a symptom, and a hopeful one in some ways. There are some hopeful young people in California who have taken my book *The White Goddess* as their Bible. They have wildwood celebrations of her, which is a definite rejection of the ordinary life that California offers. No young people who are searching for suprarational knowledge ever have any quarrel with me. I am 75; their fight is with people from 30 to 60. It's the pre-World War Two generation they're against. Take their attitude toward the computer. They have a great advantage over the middle generation, which has not, like them, been taught to think mathematically. They can take a computer by the hand and talk to it and make it do what they want. So if they wanted to bust the whole system up, they need only put the wrong plug in the wrong place and destroy millions of phony dollars, of business accounts, and the whole money ethic would go to pieces. And I'd not be too sorry to see that happen.

Playboy: How do mathematical training and computers relate to suprarational knowledge?

Graves: Mathematics and the knowledge one gets from the occult are allied. In fact, I've found in writing poetry that I have postulated major mathematical theories, including the anticipation or suspense of time. My poem *Alice,* written in about 1923, enunciated what is called in mathematics the theory of parity. Recently, I wrote a poem about *Omega*-minus—the theory underlying ideas of anti-worlds and anti-matter. You imagine a line—everything on one side is positive, everything on the other is negative. Then you can assign phenomena to one side or the other. The concept is used now as a means of out-witting the tyranny of time. I found long ago that I could suspend time while in the poetic trance, which seems to be the top level of sleep. I could capture or recapture events by forward and backward leaps of the mind. I was really where my mind was.

Playboy: Do you think young people will use this kind of suprara-tionality for the good of society?

Graves: Possibly. That depends on them. There are some bad young people. There have always been bad ones. On this island, for example, we house a whole lot of both good and bad. The police throw the bad out, the ones who can't face the reality of life here. These are the ones who come around begging for food, who steal clothes off lines and sell pot openly. They have little to offer—usually nothing more than a minor gift of playing their small handmade bamboo flutes. On the other hand, I have elsewhere met a great number of young and brilliant people in whom I have confidence, who will be able to use suprarationality for the good. These people are far from being fools; they realize what the World War Two generation doesn't: They know exactly how much dirt goes on in high places. They represent the coming cataclysm.

Playboy: What do you mean?

Graves: They will revolt against such things as the secret security police now active all over the world. They will try to restore law to its proper place. You know, law has gone right down the river. All the evil things reported from excolonial parts of the world haven't been done in the name of war but in the name of police action. Look at the war in Vietnam. First of all, it's not a war, it's a police action. That's why they have been dropping napalm and using poison. They're behaving like the police, not soldiers. I respect soldiers, real soldiers, but I seldom respect the police anywhere. They lurk behind too many governments. The evil they foster has never been so operative as now. None of the troubles plaguing the world today have been planned by decent heads of state, or heads of armies, but by men without honor who have infiltrated and taken control of the secret forces that do all the real damage and fighting.

Playboy: Why have they taken control?

Graves: Power, power, power. Evil power. Madness. Why, these people don't even particularly rejoice in their accomplishments—in other people's suffering. They can't even confess, "I've killed a man and I'm not ashamed of it." Soldiers in an honest war can at least say that. But this other sort of people lies concealed. Things can never be mentioned, never taken up, not even to get them in front of Parliament or Congress or any honest people. No, this situation is very different from war, or what we used to call war. The last honorable war was the first part of World War One, and that went to pieces in 1916.

Playboy: Why do you call the first part of that war honorable?

Graves: Well, in the case of World War One, the Germans did break a treaty. The old rule was that when nations broke their word, they had to be stopped. For a nation to lose its honor by breaking a rule or a code is the same as an individual losing his honor; therefore, the nation must suffer the consequences. However, since the Germans in that case were very strong and we were on the verge of defeat, it was only by using dishonorable means halfway through the war that we were able to win. That marked the end of old-fashioned war. Bad as wars had been, there were many cases of old-fashioned courtesy. These persisted into World War One, especially in the fraternization between English and the Germans out in no man's land in Christmas 1914. But in 1915, we were told that times had changed, that fraternization would be punishable by death. Nevertheless, two battalions who had been facing one another on the previous Christmas did get together. But even that was nearly wrecked when some bloody fool started shooting. After that incident, things got worse. The Germans had started the trouble in the spring by using poison gas, which was against international rules. But then, so also were our officers' pistols with dumdum bullets.

Playboy: Do you think there has ever been a truly good war?

Graves: There have been wars of honest defense. Also wars which were fought for fun. I'll tell you the story of one. It provides a parable for us. It was called the War of the Burnt Child and happened in New Zealand. At the time, the Maoris were awfully bored with life, because there were no wild beasts to hunt and very few sharks. The men got restless, tired of telling jokes and wrestling and playing their version of football. The malaise grew. One day, a special, very limited sort of war broke out—a sort difficult to introduce in higher civilizations, because everyone would cheat. In this case, there was a tribe whom we'll call the Cardinals. They were neighbors of another tribe we'll call the Tigers. One day the Cardinals heard of a shocking incident in the Tiger village. A man and a woman had quarreled over some trifle and upset the cooking pot, badly scalding a child. The Cardinals agreed that this was the most disgraceful thing they had ever heard of. How could a poor innocent child suffer for the stupidity and bad manners of his parents?

So the Cardinals decided they would teach the Tigers a lesson. They sent out an emissary to say, "You Tigers are a disgrace to the country. How dare you behave like this? We demand an immediate explanation, for the good of mankind." The Tigers became very cross at this and told the Cardinals to mind their own business, since the accident referred to was caused by a careless dog, not by the parents. The child was burned, true, but received great care and affection from his parents. The Tigers then demanded an apology from the Cardinals and the inevitable ensued.

The two tribes decided on war for the following Thursday. They agreed on the place and on one major rule: If anybody got killed, they had to stop. Finally, at the agreed place and hour, and after a great exchange of oratory, they clashed. It was a wonderful war— clubs bashing, lots of bruises. Finally, the Cardinals managed to subdue the Tigers, round them up and bind them. They had a tremendous victory celebration, including a feast three miles long, which meant that the eatables stretched that far along a road. Before the preparations were completed, the Cardinal chief said, "I think the

Tigers should be allowed to witness this victory celebration." So they were invited to dine and the Cardinals made speeches about the heroism of their troops, until finally their chief said, "We must praise the Tigers, too, or the victory is worthless."

Everyone became very drunk. Then came a fine idea from the Cardinal chief. He said, "And now, valiant Tigers, you understand that we have won and that your village is ours. We propose, therefore, to go there at once and live. But, since we think it shameful to make you homeless, you can have *our* village." So the Cardinals occupied the Tiger village and the Tigers occupied the Cardinal village and there was no war for a very long time.

Playboy: That sounds like a fairy tale. Can you seriously compare it with a real war?

Graves: My example points out the way civilized people who have faith in each other's honor should settle war. It took a breach of faith like that in World War One to degenerate warfare to the way it is conducted today. Another thing I would like to point out about both World Wars is that they were started by the Germans, and the Germans are a peculiar race. I know because *I* am a quarter German. The funny thing was that the Germans were once the good boys of Europe. They were the artists, the musicians, and they cleaned up the streets and brought in sterilized milk, and so on. Anyway, something happened in the 1860s. The real history has never come to light. But there was a small group who decided on a course of evil for Germany and, because the citizens were malleable, very brainwashable, they fell for it. Gradually, the rearming led to World War One, to Nazism and Hitler and World War Two.

Playboy: Don't you think there have been great men whose leadership was good?

Graves: I don't like the word great. It simply means held in public awe and esteem, and too many people are held in public awe and esteem who are not great. In my work, I have often pointed out that all the so-called great figures of the Napoleon, Hercules, Alexander type must invariably ruin the country that gave them birth. Men like them will sacrifice anything, including their own country, simply for personal power. They hold a strange fascination for their followers and that's what does the trick. I hope we won't get that anymore. Stalin is gone. He was a "great" figure who did a lot of damage.

Hitler's gone, too, though some think he's hiding out somewhere, maybe in Australia. If so, he'd be too old to do much more damage. But other people are doing the injury now—the strong evil elite who are the heads of security services. Unfortunately, they aren't always known, even by their kin.

Playboy: Is there a good elite to counteract all this evil?

Graves: Yes, there are many good people around, people who are doing a very fine job. If you'll pardon the chauvinism, the good power and influence of the queen of England is terrific. Without her, we would be right in the refuse bin.

Playboy: Why?

Graves: First, she is a woman, and a very intelligent one. Second, she is the key to the British constitution, a symbol of the Commonwealth. We've been lucky at crucial points in our history to have a queen. As we saw in the old matriarchies, female rulers always seem to behave better than kings. And, of course, there are good people who are not in the limelight. The *real* mathematicians and scientists are not known widely. Nor do they want to be, because if they do anything well publicized, they get threatened. I was talking to a cancer specialist recently. I said to him, "Are you aware of the extraordinary figures for bowel cancer in men in their 30s and 40s who happen to be nuclear physicists?" He said, "Yes, and it has nothing to do with their work in physics."

Playboy: Are you implying—or was he—that someone gave them cancer?

Graves: That's easy enough to do these days, which is why we need more good people than we have. Good people know and recognize each other. Through them the bad guys can be broken down, their policies reversed. But such goodness isn't an organized thing at all. There is merely an understanding between people when something goes wrong. The very force of that conviction is enough to break the wrong thing. Paradoxically, the evil people are few in number and really very vulnerable. Confronted by good, they recognize its power and get scared. Then they can be defeated.

Playboy: But how can we tell the good guys from the bad guys?

Graves: By the pricking of one's thumbs, Shakespeare said.

Playboy: Do you think there are good and bad nations?

Graves: I find the Dutch a very good people. They have behaved very well since they lost their empire and they behaved very well in the big wars. I am also very fond of Hungary, I suppose because they have always brought me good luck and have more poets to the square mile than any other nation in Europe. One finds poets there even among high party officials. The Hungarians, I am told, originally came from Babylonia, from which they were expelled. They retained, however, their extraordinary fineness of thought, honed by centuries of city dwelling before they were forced to become desert horsemen and eventually went down to Hungary.

Playboy: In conversation, you seem to be preoccupied with legend, myth and history. The same is even truer of your poetry, which almost never addresses itself to contemporary topics. Why?

Graves: Laura Riding said in our collaboration *A Survey of Modernist Poetry,* "Poetry must act in the vacuum left by the death of historical time to determine values." She meant that all history has already happened, that moral values are not tied to time but, rather, spring from the same magic as poetry. The trouble with people who write poems about current events is that the inspiration comes from a masculine, Apollonian, rational source. Some Americans, for example, are now expending their poetic talents on the Vietnam war. That sort of subject defeats poetry. Of course, there has always been verse based on current events, but it should be satiric. One shouldn't rant in poems against individual political situations. One can describe, in a highly personal way, how outside events are affecting one. But there must be a differentiation made in poetry between the right hand—the truly creative one—and the left, which is the satiric, destructive one. You must differentiate between satire and real poetry. Satires are needed: otherwise, one can't keep the balance between real poems and topical comment. In satire, you can say what you like; you can break all the rules of euphony in describing the threat of evil. But most of the problems I face are universal, beyond topical events and historical time. Poetry based on such universals can establish lasting values.

Playboy: How?

Graves: If it emphasizes the extreme dependence of man upon woman for her moral guidance and of woman upon man for his practical doing. Within this man-woman relationship, all values are shaped. By emphasizing and making that relationship clear, poetry can establish the important principles of life. Patriarchal or Apollonian poetry started with ballads about war. *Beowulf* and the Icelandic sagas are examples. Such poems were enough for the men of the time when they sat together in a mead hall, throwing plates and bones at each other. But they lack lasting emotional value, because they are centered on war, not love. All poetry of value is matriarchal in its origin.

Playboy: Why?

Graves: Begin with the most venerated poem in the Western world, *The Iliad.* It starts off, "Sing to me, Muse, of the anger of Achilles and its terrible consequences." The invocation of the Muse is a phrase borrowed from religious rituals which took place in such matriarchal cultures as the early Greek. The women would dance around a pile of stones which represented a phallus. They circled round and round, singing a song. They soon got worked up with the dancing and the singing and would naturally have been taking drugs, the hallucinatory mushroom laced with ivy and laurel. Finally, some-body would shriek, "Sing to me!" Then one of the dancers would become inspired exactly as in voodoo celebrations in Haiti. And, in the same way, the celebrants would know that someone was going to be "ridden" by a deity. In the matriarchal case, it was always the love goddess who possessed someone, and this someone began to sing in inspiration. So poetry originated. And Homer begins *The Iliad* that way, in order to keep the people absolutely still.

Playboy: Then you believe poetry, like drugs, creates a trance in the poet?

Graves: And, therefore in the hearer, too. An enormously impor-tant part of poetry is the incantatory and hypnotic effect. All poetry really is, or should be, hypnotic. Homer, for example, used meter to hypnotize, by recalling the dactylic steps around the sacred hermae. By using this beat, he put the audience in a state which took possession of their minds and they could understand what was be-hind the entire poem. The point about poetic meter is that it puts people into a semitrance, so that they can understand what the poet has grasped in *his* trance. All real poems are written in a trance.

Playboy: Do you mean that the poet's unconscious mind writes the poem?

Graves: I mean that he goes out of himself to magical regions.

Trance is the lightest form of sleep, a form in which you can think in a reasonable way and, at the same time, you can dredge up from your memory all the words and images you don't even know you know. All kinds of strange things appear. These images find their own rhythm and their own meter. In this state, one is really thinking in the fifth dimension. In the poetic trance, the poet can apprehend from the future as well as look into the past. That was said of the Greek poets and it's certainly true of the ancient Irish poets. My own poetry is based very squarely on the Celtic. That, in turn, is based on a very early magic which goes back as far as you like.

Playboy: Do Americans write in this tradition?

Graves: No longer. Their abandonment of incantation is one of several things wrong with American poetry. To begin with, you have been put under a trance by certain rhythmic patterns in your mind. Soon the words adapt themselves to these rhythmic patterns. But as soon as your modernists start breaking things up and scattering words and punctuation marks around the pages, they break the hypnotic order. One should always start a line with a capital letter and indent. That's enough of a command to the reader to read carefully. If he does so, and if the poem is a real one and well written, the various verse systems hidden within the poem will hypnotize both reader and poet. The poet thus brings himself to think in a way in which he does not normally think and which is really a defeat of time.

Playboy: Is there anything you like about American poetry?

Graves: Not since my friends Frost and Cummings died. When I was a student, we left English alone. We wrote verse in Latin, Greek and French to learn. So anything we wanted to do about writing English poetry, we did on our own but with a classical background. You *can't* be a poet in English, except a peasant poet, unless you're familiar with the whole history of the English language, which you can't understand without some knowledge of Latin. All but a few basic Anglo-Saxon words and a couple of key borrowings from the Spanish and the Hebrew are based on the vernacular Latin as spoken by the French, the Spaniards, the Italians or the Church.

But as for American poetry, I would say that there are more poets—more true poets linked to magic—in the remote climate of Australia than in the whole of the United States. One of the problems is that many American verse writers are paid too well. There is too much money handed out—enormous sums and prizes—for non-poems. As a result, real poets are so few that I could count them on the fingers of one hand. Look at this book I've just received from America. Nothing but typographical tricks. Poetry *concrète.*

Playboy: Yes, but on the back is this inscription: "Allen Ginsberg says this man has creative genius."

Graves: I suppose the author has said the same about Allen Ginsberg, who has a kind heart and a sense of humor but is no more a poet than my Aunt Lisa.

Playboy: Isn't his work poetry, however different it is from yours?

Graves: No. And I'm very glad to be able to talk to *Playboy* about such poets and their use of sexual subjects. To me, an important thing about sex is that, apart from farmyard animals and one or two rare exceptions such as doves, the sexual act is always performed in utter secrecy, simply because when one is engaged in it, one becomes very vulnerable. People can suddenly jump from ambush and crack one in the skull. So lovers must find someplace hidden in the middle of the woods, where they can hear people coming, or on top of a hill, where they can *see* people coming.

Therefore, because of its secret nature, you should not talk or write about sex. You can have love and sex talk with the person you're in love with—that's another matter. But any talk of sex with others is anti-human, especially if one constructs a scientology about it. There are a lot of people who write pretended love poetry but have never been in love, and the poet who has no Muse is abysmally dull. That's what is wrong with Alexander Pope and others of his contemporaries. That's what is right with John Donne. You feel the poet's original vision—it's re-created in you. A. E. Housman's test is also valid enough. He said that when a poem is truly good, the hair on the back of your neck rises. And now we're just beginning to find out about the magnetic properties of hair.

Playboy: Are there any, beyond the static electricity one gets on a comb?

Graves: Ask any trichomaniac! I'm convinced that if you cut your hair very short, as the Puritans did, you're limiting your potential for electrical discharges and receptions. If cutting your hair does limit your electrical potential, then it also probably limits your capacity for love and poetry. But aside from reading poetry of the real sort, I've

only twice had the hair rise on the back of my neck. In both cases—
very strange experiences—it occurred on a moonlit hill where there
had been pre-Christian rites.

Playboy: Tell us about them.

Graves: I had gone back in time to some primitive situation, by
what I would call the television effect. You know, you can revive
bygone scenes in some haunted houses by entering them at the same
hour and in the same sort of weather that marked the emotional
conditions of the original scene. I suppose that I judge poems by a
variation of that effect. I get in touch with the poet, his time, his mind,
the evolution of his poem. Maybe that's why there are very few poets
I can read. Most of the 18th Century is blanked out, apart from a few
unliterary ballads. But there is the rich period between John Skelton
and Shakespeare. And there are occasional poems of the early 19th
Century—such as those by Coleridge and Keats.

Playboy: Though you seem to care most about poetry, you've
devoted a great deal of time to writing novels, mythological researches, plays and short stories. Why?

Graves: Because I count all that as work and one must work to
survive. And sometimes, if some event or historic point interests me, I
regard it as my duty to write it down, usually in prose. Poetry does
not count as work somehow. It can't be planned or discovered. It
forces itself upon you without your knowing what it's all about. It
comes like the tense headache before a thunderstorm, which is
followed by an uncontrollable violence of feeling, and the whole air is
ionized. You feel absolutely wonderful when you get the first line or
two down on paper. Naturally, it takes three or four days before you
bring the poem to its final state, and even then, years later, you may
spot a word that's wrong. You know that it's been worrying you in the
back of your mind all along.

Playboy: Does rewriting ever kill the original inspiration?

Graves: No, but it often persuades you that the Muse was not
there. Her presence leaps out at you if she really was there. So do
your many mistakes. You write a poem and you find it tightening
itself up, tightening, tightening—squeezing out the last drop of water.

Playboy: As one who has centered his life and self-expression on
writing, what do you think of predictions by men such as Marshall
McLuhan that future societies will have no need for the written word?

Graves: Even if writing does disappear, there's no reason for gloom. Poetry existed long before the printed word. Long after the poems of Hesiod and Homer had been recorded, great numbers of poems were remembered and handed down orally. This still goes on in the bardic tradition, especially in Wales and Ireland. No, poetry and songs will never vanish, even if print does.

Playboy: Will poetry survive the conflict of good and evil you described earlier?

Graves: I hope so. But I'll tell you happily and cheerfully: Nothing can stop the landslide, the coming cataclysm. Nothing can stop the wide destruction of our ancient glories, amenities and pleasures. There will be a bust-up quite soon.

Playboy: Why do you say this "happily and cheerfully"?

Graves: Because it's a cataclysm that *ought* to happen. And I know that the human race will survive it. But it will be only the strong, the morally strong, who survive. I think we must trust the new generation, except for the ones who have deliberately opted out of humanity. We must trust the ones who manage to stay in, to stay alive and struggling—young people especially, who have not been corrupted by the intervening generation. They will survive because they will know what they're up against. So I'm not frightened about the world ending. A few nuclear devices may explode and cause immense danger. But we will then be fortunate that the whole loveless system will have given way in a general breakdown. And if good fortune is with us—who knows?—it may be replaced by something at least no worse.

A Meeting with Robert Graves

Dannie Abse/1972

From *Encounter,* 60 (February 1983), 53-6. Reprinted by permission.

I think Sam Wanamaker, the American-born actor, sometimes stands at a window of his house in Southwark, Bankside, and sees his immediate environs not as they now are but as they were in Shakespeare's time. Certainly he imagines Southwark as it may be in the future, as it ought to be. Mr. Wanamaker's vision is that of a Bankside once again thriving, bustling with denizens of London in search of serious entertainment—the Globe Playhouse itself, reconstructed. To realise that vision Sam Wanamaker formed the Globe Theatre Centre and since 1972 has encouraged contemporary poets, each year, to honour on the page and on the platform the supreme poet and dramatist of all time. For one of the centre's commendable aims was, and is, "to create a Shakespeare Birthday Fund which will commission new works of music, poetry, drama and art to be presented annually as the most appropriate tribute to Shakespeare's memory."

In April 1972 Sam Wanamaker accordingly planned a concert in Southwark Cathedral. Nine contemporary composers were commissioned to contribute music, thirteen contemporary poets to write poems and speak them. I remember being somewhat pleased *and* worried when Christopher Hampton, on Mr. Wanamaker's behalf, asked me to be one of the poets—pleased because Mr. Hampton had invited, or intended to invite, a number of poets including W. H. Auden and Robert Graves whom I admired but had not met and now would meet; worried because I knew that poetry is something that cannot be willed, that I could not will a poem into existence, that I might not be able to keep a promise to provide a new poem for the occasion. As Shelley once wrote, 'Poetry is not like reasoning, a power to be converted according to the determination of the will. A man cannot say, 'I will compose poetry.' The greatest poet even cannot say it; for the mind in creation is as a fading coal, which some

168

invisible influence, like an inconstant wind, awakens to transitory brightness. . . . " Nevertheless, persuaded by Christopher Hampton, I accepted the commission and eventually, armed with a new poem, I went along to Southwark Cathedral to read it.

I suppose many of us have wished sometimes, frail and silly wishes, that we could turn back the clock, be transported if only for an instant to a certain place, at a certain time. Driving over towards Southwark, I wished uselessly that I could have attended a Shakespeare play at the original Globe Theatre—perhaps *Julius Caesar*, for I had read a description by a Thomas Platter of an evening at the Globe when he saw that play. "After dinner, at about two o'clock, I went with my party across the water", wrote Thomas Platter. "In the straw-thatched house we saw the tragedy of the first Emperor Julius Caesar, very pleasantly performed, with approximately fifteen characters; at the end of the play they danced together admirably and exceedingly gracefully, according to their custom, two in each group dressed in men's and two in women's apparel." Yes, it would have been interesting to have travelled across the water in that party; as a guest from another century it would be like being a stranger in a foreign land.

Instead I drove through 20th-century London towards London Bridge in my Austin 1300. It was a lovely, fresh April day; it was good to be alive. Soon, before me lay Southwark Cathedral where that afternoon I would discover, I hoped, one more sweet beginning and no unsavoury end. I parked the car, then walked into the cathedral to meet, at once, Christopher Hampton who told me that Cecil Day Lewis was seriously ill, was in fact dying; also that W. H. Auden would not be with us for he was in New York.

"You'll be reading your poem in the second half, after an interval", Christopher said. "Is that all right? Let me show you where I want you to sit."

As I followed Christopher I saw, near the door in the north aisle of the nave, Sam Wanamaker talking to Stephen Spender, Peter Porter, and an elderly man whom I did not know. Could it be Robert Graves, I wondered.

"Yes", said Christopher, "he looks pretty fit, doesn't he? He's seventy-six now, you know."

I recalled Graves's own self-portrait:

Crookedly broken nose—low tackling caused it;
Cheeks, furrowed; coarse grey hair, flying
                                                    frenetic;
Forehead, wrinkled and high;
Jowls, prominent; ears, large; jaw, pugilistic;
Teeth, few; lips, full and ruddy; mouth ascetic.
I paused with razor poised, scowling derision
At the mirrored man whose beard needs my
                                                    attention
And once more ask him why
He still stands ready, with a boy's presumption,
To court the queen in her high silk pavilion.

His face had softened with age evidently, but he still looked sprightly
enough to chase that same queen and catch her. In the choir stalls
Christopher pointed to the seat he wanted me to occupy, immediately after the interval. "Between Graves and Adrian Mitchell, all
right?"

I had liked Robert Graves's poetry for many years: it was always well-
organized and lucid, always an internally directed soliloquy that the
reader, as it were, was privileged to overhear. He composed poems in
the central English lyric tradition and he used a conservative diction
and a logical syntax without display, though not without the power to
surprise. His was an essentially romantic sensibility with its belief in
phantoms and miracles, in the terrifying and terrific supernatural; in
his interest in myth as a living, operative power even in our so-called
rational societies; and not least in his preoccupation with the creative
and destructive element that waxes and wanes in a man-woman
relationship. Yes, I looked forward to meeting Robert Graves;
besides, his reputation as a man was intriguing. I had heard how he
could be iconoclastic, anti-academic; how he was quick to deflate
lofty pretensions, how he could be wittily bitchy about his most
celebrated contemporaries.
   I was introduced to him in the Harvard Chapel, which lay behind
the north choir aisle, as the buzzing audience were returning to their
seats in the nave after the interval. "John Harvard", Robert Graves
told me, was baptised here in 1607." I assumed John Harvard was
the gentleman who emigrated to Massachusetts to make a fortune
and to found Harvard College. I was not sure, though, and not

wishing to boob I said nothing. Soon Robert Graves was telling me, as we took our seats in the choir, all kinds of esoteric information about the cathedral. He seemed anxious to instruct me. My knowledge of the cathedral was small, my ignorance large—and even if I should have dared to pronounce on that which I did know, it would have been without confidence, like a blind man naming the colours in a rainbow. Instead, I told him the names of the poets who one by one, faced the very large audience, for he was most eager to identify them. "Who's that?" he would spit out to me.

"Vernon Scannell", I'd say and as soon as Vernon had finished his poem and the next piece of music commenced—by Richard Rodney Bennett or Lennox Berkeley or Peter Maxwell Davies or John Tavener—Robert Graves would generously impart to me his next small piece of scholarship: "Edward Shakespeare, William's youngest brother, was buried in the churchyard here." He pulled out a snuffbox, an antique, from his pocket and surreptitiously showed it to me. I learnt a few quick facts about that snuffbox, its provenance, before the music ended. "Who's that?" asked Robert Graves a minute later. "Peter Redgrove," I said.

For the next twenty minutes we bartered information for information. His numerous facts for my one name. He mentioned Hollar's drawing of the Bankside three centuries past and I believe if the musical pieces had been more prolonged I would have learnt of "the colouring of Titian, the grace of Raphael, the purity of Domenichino, the *corregiescity* of Correggio, the learning of Poussin, the airs of Guido, the taste of the Carracci, or the grand contours of Michelangelo." I began to feel that my contribution to the whispered dialogue was insufficient. I tried to think of some relevant piece of recondite information *I* could drop; but all I could think of was a conversation I had once with a man who worked at London Zoo who had told me that tortoises often died of diphtheria. Somehow, to state baldly there and then, "Tortoises frequently die because of diphtheroid organisms in their throat", did not seem right and proper.

In any event, suddenly, a whole group of strangers descended upon us and began to sing a song for Shakespeare's birthday, 1972. Robert Graves seemed pleased: he had written the words for it. We both listened intently as a maniacal conductor waved his arms and the choir *so near, so loud,* sang:

When Will sat forging plays with busy friends
He wrote no worse than they;
When he sat writing for his loves, and us,
Such play outshone all play.
And still it does today.

I had the sense *not* to say, "That was pretty awful." I smiled like a hypocrite when the audience applauded enthusiastically as the immoderate choir scurried away and Robert Graves stood to his feet. He raised two hands like a triumphant boxer who had knocked his opponent out. It was certainly hard to think of him as one aged seventy-six. Back in his corner, I mean his seat, he whispered to me, "That was the best thing we've heard all afternoon."

"Who's that?" Robert Graves asked.

"George McBeth", I replied.

Eventually it was my turn to walk the twenty-two yards to the scaffold and face all those seated figures in the soaring, elongated nave (rebuilt, I think Robert Graves said, in 1897 to replace the, er, 13th-century nave destroyed, er, in 1838). It is not easy to read one poem only. As soon as you become used to the stressful situation, the hundreds of upturned faces, the different sources of light, the un-friendly microphone, the whole thing is over. You have been bowled out, the audience are clapping out of habit but you are walking back to the pavilion pulling off your batting gloves; knowing that you have made a duck. I sat down and took my own pulse.

Music began—by Harrison Birtwhistle.

Robert Graves leaned over towards me. I thought he was going to say, "Well done", or "That was a good poem"—something sensible like that. Instead he whispered more confidentially, "He nodded at me, you know."

"What?" I asked, wondering.

"He nodded at me."

"Who?"

"The Prime Minister."

I paused. When I was reading, I had spotted someone in the front row, in spitting distance, a man with a red, adipose, shining face who did, come to think of it, look very familiar.

"Edward Heath?" I asked.

"Of course", Robert Graves said irritably, as if I were a dunce and did not know with certainty even the name of the present Prime Minister.

For my part, I felt irritated with Robert Graves. He was supposed to be a rebel, a nonconformist; and now here he was full of ridiculous pride, *hubris*, because the Prime Minister, a *Tory* Prime Minister (whom, of course, *I* did not vote for), had nodded at him.

"What did you do?" I whispered.

"I nodded back", Robert Graves said.

At this point, Adrian Mitchell who had just arrived, late—at least he looked as if he had just parked his motorbike at the south transept door—took the empty seat on my left-hand side.

"Adrian", I said quietly, "Mr. Graves is on nodding terms with our Prime Minister."

I explained to Adrian that the Prime Minister was sitting in the front row. This information activated Adrian Mitchell—his skin, eyes, horns altered. "Is Heath here?" hissed Adrian between bared teeth, his face contorted, vivid with displeasure. Evidently Adrian regarded Heath as an amalgam of Caligula and Hitler.

Just then Birtwhistle's music ceased and the audience applauded again.

"Yes", said Robert Graves benignly, cheerful, leaning over me toward Adrian Mitchell, "Mr. Heath's sitting in the front row." But now it was Adrian's turn to read his poem. He almost ran toward the microphone.

"Who's that?" asked Robert Graves, startled.

There are those who hardly know what they think until they express it either vocally or on the page. That is not true of Adrian Mitchell. His political views are not shaded. They inform and energise his work, they translate him as a man, they draw him, as it were, as clearly as a pencil can draw a profile. I have a feeling that Adrian perceived no human being occupying that chair in the front row but a monstrous cartoon figure, one responsible for all the treachery in the world, all the injustice, coercion, easy manipulation, casual greed, inequality, unnecessary pain. Now, at last, here was a chance of a lifetime to confront bluntly that one who had previously stood in the shadow, that cartoon figure, that prime adversary. Adrian boiled with rage. He began to abuse Edward Heath, accused him of being partly

responsible for the chemical warfare in Viet Nam, and those at the
back of the nave, far away, clapped while those somewhat wealthier,
in front, nearer to the presence of the Prime Minister, sat dumbly.
Then Adrian Mitchell read his poem and afterwards, in reverse,
curiously pale, rushed past us through the choir to disappear down
the south transept whence he had come.

Some music started up—by Elizabeth Lutyens, I think—and
Robert Graves said, "You've seen the tomb of Lancelot Andrewes?
He was buried originally in the Bishop's Chapel, you know."

The concert was almost over, this was the last musical composition
and all the poets had read their commissioned poems. Sam Wanamaker had arranged for the concert to conclude with a reading by
the actress Diane Cilento. She had been asked to recite the epitaph
by John Milton on the Admirable Dramatick Poet, W. Shakespeare.
The attractive blond actress moved to the microphone and I
happened to glance at Robert Graves who seemed to be following
her progress with exceptional interest—rather, I thought, as the
elderly King David must have looked upon, for the first time, the
beautiful Abishag. Before the microphone Miss Cilento recited
without book:

> What needs my Shakespeare for his honour'd bones
> The labour of an age in piled stones?
> Or that his hallow'd reliques should be hid
> Under a starry pointing pyramid? . . .
> What need'st thou such weak witness of thy name?
>
> Thou, in our wonder and astonishment
> Hast built thyself a live-long monument . . . .

The Milton poem, over, Diane Cilento bowed to the applauding
audience with pleasing grace. "Who's that?" asked Robert Graves
once more.

"Diane Cilento," I told him.

Robert Graves hesitated, furrowed his brows, nodded his head.

"Cilento," he said.

"Yes."

"Cilento. Quite a gifted poet," he said.

"She's an actress," I explained.

"An actress?" he asked.

"The poem was by Milton."

"Quite. Ah yes, I thought that poem sounded familiar."

I did not laugh. Robert Graves had made the sort of boob that I could have made. I looked at him with growing affection; he looked at me, puzzled.

Later, at the reception that followed the concert, near the entrance, I met Sam Wanamaker. "Let me introduce you to Robert Graves," he said. I looked across the crowded room and saw Mr. Graves deep in dialogue with Mr. Heath. "It's okay," I said. "We've met. In fact, we've had quite an intermittent, instructive conversation. We both enjoyed the music so much."

The Graves I Know

James Reeves/1975

From *The Malahat Review*, 33 (1975), 14-8. Reprinted by permission.

I first met Robert Graves when he was forty. I last met him when he was seventy-nine. In a sense the title of these reflections should therefore be, rather, "The Graveses I know" for a complicated and controversial man has many sides. Nevertheless, as I turn back the leaves of memory, I will try to give a consistent picture of the essential Robert as he exists for me. What first attracted me to his poems was their Englishness, their feeling for the whole tradition of native English poetry from the old ballads and Skelton to our own time—Hardy, De la Mare, Blunden, Owen and some Americans, notably John Crowe Ransom and Robert Frost. As a companion with whom to read and discuss poetry he is unrivalled. As a disputant in the press, he has always been fair, good-humoured, entertaining and cogent—a fact mentioned to me with delight by Donald Davie when the two were in controversy. Entering into all he has said to me over these forty years is his vivid personality: I would call it a personality of intellect, not of will or persuasion or yet of compulsion. I have always resisted compulsion, feeling compelled only by what does not try to compel. From the first I respected Robert's knowledge, because it was always germane to the central interest of his being, the Englishness of his achievement. This is true even of the marginal bits of his knowledge and interest. If he picked up an odd fact, a bit of something in a junk shop, an *objet trouvé* on the beach, it became a part of him. His houses in Majorca, as they were in England when he lived here, are full of such extensions of his personality.

His intellect informs his judgments and gives them authority—not simply literary judgments, but judgments of people and things. He has no patience with the pretentious and the spurious. This quality is reflected in his poems, whose rejection of what is factitious and showy is an example to us all. As a young writer, this was invaluable to me. Robert always had two things which I could only envy and have not had the energy or the power to emulate until late in life—his industry, which, during all the earlier and middle years of our friendship, was tireless; and his craftmanship, which in the best of his poems is impeccable. Rhythms which combine the sound of natural English speech with the basic iambic movement of traditional English poetry; rhymes which are inevitable and do not demand a distortion of the natural word-order; syntax which is correct without being obtrusive; economy without obscurity—these are the attractive qualities of his technique—which is to say nothing of the saltiness of his diction and the wry pithiness of his thought. *Lost Acres* comes to mind as one of his best and most characteristic poems—a belief which I found I shared with another of Graves' earliest admirers, William Empson, who, like me, regretted its omission from Robert's own Penguin selection.

Some of Robert's ideas—even occasionally, though seldom, about poetry—have struck me as wrong. For instance, Nevill Coghill and I were obliged to point out to him, after an Oxford lecture in which he said there was no such being as a male Muse, that Shakespeare's sonnets, to go no further, gave him the lie. It is fair to say that, in conversation with Robert on his seventy-ninth birthday, he seemed to me to have changed that view. Some of his ideas about other things, like magic and oriental philosophy, have seemed to me barmy. But that has nothing to do with the essential integrity of his thinking and his personality at its most authoritative. In eighty years of continuous growth, his mind has taken in what I would call the outer wards of emotional and intellectual experience, and here a man is entitled to be erratic, unreasonable and even, by others' standards, wrong. For me, such excursions merely point up the central and authoritative rightness of the real Graves, poet and man.

Poet and man: essentially there is and can be no distinction. His characteristic poems are well wrought, clearly observed, grotesque, witty, wholly experienced and completely original—such poems as *Lost Acres, Lollocks, On Being, To Juan at the Winter Solstice, To Bring the Dead to Life, On Dwelling, The Cool Web, The Bards, The Legs, The Laureate* and *Flying Crooked*. By these, to write like a reviewer, his reputation is secured. As poet and man, one of his most admired gifts is that of concentration, a total exclusion of every

outward distraction which could break the trance in which he is
dwelling on the problem uppermost in his mind. He uses a friend or
a companion as an audience for his reflections. To walk with him
anywhere, but especially in the neighborhood of his longtime home
in Majorca, is to be continuously aware of his concentration: he
misses nothing in the context, visual or audible, of his contemplation.
The increasing noisiness of life has driven him gradually more into
himself. I am inclined to think that he would regard commercial
entertainment on the air as the biggest single enemy.

These reflections have taken me back to when I first knew him in
Deyá, the village which has been his home for more than half his life.
They have also taken me back in memory to Galmpton, near Dart-
mouth, his first home with his wife Beryl, after his return from
America just before World War II. Somehow, despite obvious differences, he made Galmpton into Deyá. The war period began for me a
new lease of friendship, a friendship which has grown to include
Beryl and their four children, and now their four grandchildren. My
wife and I, and later our children and grand-children, have been
enriched by this warm and varied friendship, and rewarded by many
common interests and concerns. Ever since my children were young
visitors to Deyá, we have been vividly conscious of the generosity of
spirit and lavish hospitality we have experienced there. It is as if
Robert and his family live to give. From Robert the giving is not only
material, it is in companionship, encouragement, advice, consolation,
correspondence.

However long Deyá lasts—and it still looks solid and permanent—
Robert will always be ambling back and forth among the olives, the
shut cool houses, the antique terraces. He will never be, however,
what his whole life has been a protest against becoming—a ghost.
Poetic unreason, his special province and the title of an early book,
will see to that. Deyá forty years after is to me astonishingly
unchanged. True, there are piped water, milk, electricity in plenty, as
there were not in 1935; there are cars, as there were not then; there
are plastics, Coca-Cola, canned music and other amenities. But the
heart of the village is still the same. If I were suddenly to be set down
there, I would recognize it instantly, even if I had not visited it more
than once in the fifties. In some ways it is a better place for an aging
man like me with little eyesight. Prosperity has made everyday life

easier, lighter, more varied. Deyá's centre, the great hill surmounted
by the high church, approached by winding streets of small, compact
houses, is immutable. Morning glory still ramps over the walls. The
little bay where we have lunch and bathe is scarcely changed. We
drink the same *vin de pompe* at the two cafés, smoke the same
harsh, black cigarettes, talk the higher trivialities of life, art and politics
with the same assorted visitors from Europe and America. Now
Robert's and Beryl's children have grown up. William's job takes him
to Scotland, Lucia's and Ramon's to Barcelona. But by good fortune
my 1974 holiday coincided with visits by all four. Among them
Robert moved abstractedly, recovering from an operation. Beryl and
the others seemed to me to radiate the same warmth and brilliance
that come from the hot sky, from the water of the Mediterranean,
whose colour there is pure E Major, Mozart's most nostalgic key, and
from the walls of honey-coloured stone, varied in tone and texture as
a gathering of loved voices and faces. The inconvenience of thinking
about too much beauty and generosity is that it reduces me to tears.
And I have left unsaid half of what I would like to have said.

Robert Graves at Deyá

Jorge Luis Borges/1985

From *The New York Review of Books* (August 15, 1985), 20.
Reprinted by permission. Translated by Anthony Kerrigan.

As I write these lines, perhaps even as you read them, Robert Graves, beyond time and free of its dates and numbers, is dying in Mallorca. He is in the throes of death but not agonizing, for agony implies struggle. Nothing further from struggle and closer to ecstasy than that seated old man surrounded in his immobility by his wife, children, and grandchildren, the youngest on his knee, and a variety of pilgrims from different parts of the world (one of them a Persian, I believe). The tall body continued faithful to its functions, though he did not see or hear or utter a word: his was a soul alone. I thought he could not make us out, but when I said goodbye he shook my hand and kissed Maria Kodama's hand. At the garden gate his wife said: "You must come back! This is heaven!" That was in 1981. We went back in 1982. His wife was feeding him with a spoon; everyone was sad and awaited the end. I am aware that these dates are, for him, a single eternal instant.

The reader will not have forgotten *The White Goddess;* I will recall here the gist of one of Graves' own poems.

Alexander did not die in Babylon at the age of thirty-two. After a battle he becomes lost and for many nights makes his way through the wilderness. Finally he descries the campfires of a bivouac. Yellow, slant-eyed men take him in, succor him, and finally enlist him in their army. Faithful to his lot as a soldier, he serves in long campaigns across deserts which form a part of a geography unknown to him. A day arrives on which the troop is paid off. He recognizes his own profile on a silver coin and says to himself: *This is from the medal I had struck to celebrate the victory at Arbela when I was Alexander of Macedon.*

This fable deserves to be very ancient.

Index